THE QUOTABLE WALKER

The
Quotable
Walker

*Great Moments
of Wisdom and Inspiration
for Walkers and Hikers*

Edited by
ROGER GILBERT,
JEFFREY ROBINSON,
and
ANNE WALLACE

BREAKAWAY BOOKS
HALCOTTSVILLE, NY
2000

THE QUOTABLE WALKER:
Great Moments of Wisdom and Inspiration for Walkers and Hikers

Compilation and preface copyright © 2000
by Roger Gilbert, Jeffrey Robinson, and Anne Wallace

All photographic images courtesy of Photodisc.com

ISBN: 1-891369-22-9
Library of Congress Control Number: 00-133191

Published by BREAKAWAY BOOKS
P.O. Box 24
Halcottsville, NY 12438
(800) 548-4348
(212) 898-0408
Visit our website at **www.breakawaybooks.com**

Distributed by Consortium Book Sales & Distribution

FIRST EDITION

CONTENTS

PREFACE

Walking—as basic a human activity as breathing and eating and sleeping—why would anyone bother writing about it? Like breathing, it becomes transparent, invisible; it's just a way of getting from here to there, the fiber optics of a phone conversation, the pipeline that brings us the oil. To talk or write about walking?—how unnecessary! how . . . pedestrian!

And yet over the centuries hundreds of walkers, like the nineteenth-century essayist Leslie Stephen, have written "In Praise of Walking," describing their experiences on foot with pleasure and bewilderment, wondering at the world around them and at themselves. This instinctive physiological movement seems to create a desire to promote, defend, explore, admire, and occasionally to scoff at itself. Walking's inarticulate, elemental nature becomes the occasion for outpourings of words about such abstract matters as civilization, ethics, the nature of the self, and the moral structure of the universe. Imagine being passionate about walking! And yet these writers are—as you may already be, if you are reading *The Quotable Walker*.

Who but a lover of walking would observe one "brushing ankle-deep in flowers"? or would tell or ask us:

> every morning
> > I stroll out into the fields,
> > > I believe in everything—

or

> > In the platinum forest walked a white maiden

or

> > What is death where there are no more roads?

Walking has become much more than just a means of locomotion; we know it as a pleasure, a recreation, a sport . . . which is how its literature rightly has found a path to the door of Breakaway Books. It is an activity long associated with the health of the body and the spirit. It parts company with most sports in that competition, against either others or oneself, is not terribly important; nor has sports technology particularly influenced walking, with the minor exception of the manufacture of light, well-cushioned, and ventilated shoes. So those who write about walking haven't been so interested in feats of strength and speed, or in analyzing and promoting tactics and instructions for making the body the perfect walking instrument. Rather, they connect walking with living well—physically, perceptively, imaginatively, spiritually, ethically. Obviously walking is good exercise, but the health of the walker—according to those who witness and experience it—is "whole-souled." This is why so much walking literature exists, why it has occupied the minds of such a range of personalities; it is why so much of it, while intent on explaining itself, still leaves room for the thoughts of its individual readers.

Your three editors have written books on the literature of walking, a fact that brought them together for *The Walker's Literary Companion* (Breakaway Books). Compiling that collection of poems, fiction, and essays left us at once with a sense of delight and frustration: delight in having brought between covers the wonderful and varied literature of walking, and frustration at not being able to include more of equal interest. *The Quotable Walker* has allowed us to present many more instances of walkers' praise of their pastime. Over the past 100 years walkers have put together a small but substantial number of anthologies of walking literature (*The Walker's Literary Companion* being the most recent and, we think, the largest and most wide-ranging), but no one has yet collected an entire book of quotations on walking, a treasury, a kind of bank vault of literary gems on the subject, the best-kept secrets of ambulators.

The quotation, of course, differs from an essay or poem in its brevity and its fragmentary nature. So you may think of a quotation about walking as a single step on a path, a step that may open into full praise or into its own world of thought. We offer some ideas about where these paths might lead by grouping quotations around the different purposes and occasions of walking, and by heading each section with a guiding epigraph, a quotation that we think suggests the thought-direction of that section. But before any guiding purpose, the following passages—culled from world literature—are chosen to bring to you the reader, like walking itself, moments of pleasure.

Roger Gilbert   Jeffrey Robinson   Anne Wallace

Precepts and Instructions

I have met with but one or two persons in the course of my life who understood the art of Walking, that is, of taking walks—who had a genius, so to speak, for sauntering: which word is beautifully derived "from idle people who roved about the country, in the Middle Ages, and asked charity, under pretense of going à la Sainte Terre," to the Holy land, till the children exclaimed, "There goes a Sainte-Terrer," a Saunterer, a Holy-Lander.

—**Henry David Thoreau**, "Walking"

A journey of a thousand miles begins with a single step.
—*Tao Te Ching*

The longest journey begins with a single step, not with a turn of the ignition key. That's the best thing about walking, the journey itself. It doesn't much matter whether you get where you're going or not. You'll get there anyway. Every good hike brings you eventually back home. Right where you started.

—**Edward Abbey,** "Walking"

With the first step, the number of shapes the walk might take is infinite, but then the walk begins to "define" itself as it goes along, though freedom remains total with each step: any tempting side-road can be turned into on impulse, or any wild patch of woods can be explored. The pattern of the walk is to come true, is to be recognized, discovered.

—**A. R. Ammons,** "A Poem Is a Walk"

Isn't it really quite extraordinary to see that, since man took his first step, no one has asked himself why he walks, how he walks, if he has ever walked, if he could walk better, what he achieves in walking . . . questions that are tied to all the philosophical, psychological, and political systems which preoccupy the world.

—**Honoré de Balzac,** *Theorie de la Demarché*

✪

The book of Nature is that which the physician must read; and to do so he must walk over the leaves.

—**Paracelsus**

✪

Better! A rare strong, hearty, healthy walk—four statute miles an hour—preferable to that rumbling, tumbling, jolting, shaking, scraping, creaking, villainous old gig? Why, the two things will not admit of comparison. It is an insult to the walk, to set them side by side. Where is an instance of a gig having ever circulated a man's blood, unless when, putting him in danger of his neck, it awakened in his veins and in his ears, and all along his spine, a tingling heat, much more peculiar than agreeable? When did a gig ever sharpen anybody's wits and energies, unless it was when the horse bolted, and, crashing madly down a steep hill with a stone wall at the bottom, his desperate circumstances suggested to the only gentleman left inside, some novel and unheard-of mode of dropping out behind? Better than the gig!

—**Charles Dickens,** *Martin Chuzzlewit*

In my room, the world is beyond my understanding.
But when I walk I see that it consists of three or four hills
    and a cloud.

—**Wallace Stevens,** "Of the Surface of Things"

WALK in the world
(you can't see anything
from a car window, still less
from a plane, or from the moon!? Come
off of it.)

—**William Carlos Williams,** *Paterson*

Only he who walks the road on foot learns of the power it commands, and of how, from the very scenery that for the flier is only the unfurled plain, it calls forth distances, belvederes, clearings, prospects at each of its turns like a commander deploying soldiers at the front.

—**Walter Benjamin,** "One Way Street"

The walks are the unobtrusive connecting thread of other memories, and yet each walk is a little drama itself, with a definite plot with episodes and catastrophes, according to the requirements of Aristotle; and it is naturally interwoven with all the thoughts, the friendships, and the interests that form the staple of ordinary life.

—**Leslie Stephen,** "In Praise of Walking"

There are many schools of walking and none of them orthodox.

—**George Macaulay Trevelyan,** "Walking"

It is a gentle art; know how to tramp and you know how to live.   —**Stephen Graham,** "The Gentle Art of Tramping"

It is a fact that not once in all my life have I gone out for a walk. I have been taken out for walks; but that is another matter. Even while I trotted prattling by my nurse's side I regretted the good old days when I had, and wasn't, a perambulator.
—**Max Beerbohm,** "Going Out for a Walk"

He who sits still in a house all the time may be the greatest vagrant of all; but the saunterer, in the good sense, is no more vagrant than the meandering river, which is all the while sedulously seeking the shortest course to the sea.
—**Henry David Thoreau,** "Walking"

To walk because it is good for you warps the soul, just as it warps the soul for a man to talk for hire or because he thinks it his duty.

—**Hilaire Belloc,** Introduction to *The Footpath Way*

One must walk all the things of life about which one talked.

—**Robert Creeley,** *A Day Book*

If you want to talk the talk you've got to walk the walk.

—**Proverbial**

What one cannot fly over, he must limp around.

—**Johann Wolfgang von Goethe,** *Faust*

The history of mankind is the instant
between two strides taken by a traveler.

—**Franz Kafka,** *Notebooks*

One step in the snow is enough to shake the mountain.
—**Edmond Jabes,** *The Little Book of Unsuspected Subversion*

New myths are born beneath each of our steps.
—**Louis Aragon,** *Nightwalker*

I cannot see, as I hurry along, what could constitute for me, even without my knowing it, a magnetic pole in either space or time.
—**Andre Breton,** *Nadja*

A walk is just one more layer, a mark laid upon the thousands of other layers of human and geographic history on the surface of the land.

A walk traces the surface of the land, it follows an idea, it follows the day and the night.
—**Richard Long,** "Five Six Pick Up Sticks, Seven Eight Lay Them Straight"

A walk is all about wind and bottom.
—**Adam Nicolson,** *On Foot*

A walk is not a straight line, but a zigzag through time.
—**Joan Connor,** "Tidal Walk"

I will try
to fasten into order enlarging grasps of disorder,
widening
scope, but enjoying the freedom that
Scope eludes my grasp, that there is no finality of vision,
that I have perceived nothing completely,
that tomorrow a new walk is a new walk.
—**A. R. Ammons,** "Corsons Inlet"

But why tramp? Are there not railroads and Pullmans
enough, that you must walk? That is what a great many of
my friends said when they learned of my determination to

travel from Ohio to California on foot; and very likely it is the question that will first come to your mind in reading of the longest walk for pure pleasure that is on record. . . . I was after neither time nor money, but life—not life in the pathetic meaning of the poor health-seeker, for I was perfectly well and a trained athlete; but life in the truer, broader, sweeter sense, the exhilarant joy of living outside the sorry fences of society, living with a perfect body and a wakened mind.

—**Charles F. Lummis,** *A Tramp Across the Continent*

Walking is a universal form of exercise, not age-oriented or bound to any national heritage, and it costs and implies nothing except maybe a tolerant heart. Like other sports, it calls for a good eye as well as cheerful legs—those chunky gluteus muscles that are the butt of mankind's oldest jokes—because the rhythm of walking is in the sights and one's response as much as simply in how one steps. In America at the moment it may seem like something of a reader's or an individualist's sport, because we are becoming suburban, and the suburbs have not yet adjusted to the avocation of walking. But they will.

—**Edward Hoagland,** "City Walking"

But strange things do happen when you trudge twenty miles a day, day after day, month after month. Things you only become totally conscious of in retrospect. For one thing I had remembered in minute and Technicolor detail everything that had happened in my past and all the people who belonged there. I had remembered every word of every conversation I had had or overheard way, way back in my childhood and in this way I had been able to review these events, with a kind of emotional detachment as if they had happened to somebody else. I was rediscovering and getting to know people who were long since dead and forgotten. . . . And I was happy, there is simply no other word for it.

—**Robyn Davidson,** *Tracks*

Distance changes utterly when you take the world on foot. A mile becomes a long way, two miles literally considerable, ten miles whopping, fifty miles at the very limits of conception. The world, you realize, is enormous in a way that only you and a small community of fellow hikers know. Planetary scale is your little secret.

—**Bill Bryson,** *A Walk in the Woods*

When pilgrims begin to walk several things usually begin to happen to their perceptions of the world which continue over the course of their journey: they develop a changing sense of time, a heightening of the senses, and a new awareness of their bodies and the landscape. . . . A young German man expressed it this way: "In the experience of walking, each step is a thought. You can't escape yourself."

—**Nancy Frey,** *Pilgrim Stories*

Some days I think this one place isn't enough. That's when nothing is enough, when I want to live multiple lives and have the know-how and guts to love without limits. Those days, like today, I walk with a purpose but no destination. Only then do I see, at least momentarily, that most everything is here. To my left a towering cottonwood is lunatic with bird song. Under it, I'm a listening post while its great, gray trunk—like a baton—heaves its green symphony into the air.

—**Gretel Ehrlich,** "Looking for a Lost Dog"

✦

After a day's walk everything has twice its usual value.
—**George Macaulay Trevelyan,** "Walking"

✦

It is good to collect things; it is better to take walks.
—**Anatole France**

Legs, Feet, and Footwear

I have two doctors, my left leg and my right. When body and mind are out of gear (and those twin parts of me live at such close quarters that the one always catches melancholy from the other) I know that I have only to call in my doctors and I shall be well again.

—**George Macaulay Trevelyan,** "Walking"

What creature goes on four legs in the morning, two legs in the afternoon, and three legs in the evening?
   —**The riddle of the Sphinx**

❂

The goddess can be recognized by her step.
   —**Virgil,** *Aeneid*

❂

Watt's way of advancing due east, for example, was to turn his bust as far as possible towards the north and at the same time to fling out his right leg as far as possible towards the south, and then again to turn his bust as far as possible towards the south and at the same time to fling out his left leg as far as possible towards the north, and then again to turn his bust as far as possible towards the north and to fling out his right leg as far as possible towards the south, and then again to turn his bust as far as possible towards the south and to fling out his left leg as far as possible towards the north, and so on, over and over again, many many times, until he reached his destination, and could sit down. So standing first on one leg, and then on the other, he moved forward, a headlong tardigrade, in a straight line. The knees, on these occasions, did not bend. They could have, but did not. No knees could better bend than Watt's, when they chose, there was nothing the matter with Watt's knees, as may appear. But when out walking they did not bend, for some obscure reason. Notwithstanding this, the feet fell, heel and sole together, flat upon the ground, and left it, for the air's uncharted ways, with manifest repugnancy. The arms were content to dangle, in perfect equipendency.

—**Samuel Beckett,** *Watt*

Well, this is what I mean by dancing in daily life. For myself, I think the walk of New Yorkers is amazingly beautiful, so large and clear. But when I go inland, or out West, it is much sweeter. On the other hand, it has very little either of Caribbean lusciousness or of Italian *contraposto*. It hasn't much savor, to roll on your tongue, that it hasn't. Or at least you have to be quite subtle, or very much in love to distinguish so delicate a perfume.

...I can't expect you to see my point without having been to countries where the way of walking is quite different from what ours is here. However, if you were observant, and you ought to be as dance majors, you would have long ago enjoyed the many kinds of walking you can see right in this city, boys and girls, Negro and white, Puerto Rican and Western American and Eastern, foreigners, professors and dancers, mechanics and businessmen, ladies entering a theater with half a drink too much, and shoppers at Macy's.

—**Edwin Denby,** "Dancers, Buildings, and People in the Streets"

Rhythm is originally the rhythm of the feet. Every human being walks, and since he walks on two legs with which he strikes the ground in turn and since he only moves if he continues to do this, whether intentionally or not, a rhythmic sound ensues.

—**Elias Canetti,** *Crowds and Power*

There's all sorts of walking—from heading out across the desert in a straight line to a sinuous weaving through undergrowth. Descending rocky ridges and talus slopes is a specialty in itself. It is an irregular dancing—always shifting—step of walk on slabs and scree. The breath and eye are always following the uneven rhythm. It is never paced or clocklike, but flexing—little jumps—going for the well-seen place to put a foot on a rock, hit flat, move on—zigzagging along and all deliberate. The alert eye looking ahead, picking the footholds to come, while never missing the step of the moment. The body-mind is so at one with this rough world that it makes these moves effortlessly once it has had a bit of practice. The mountain keeps up with the mountain.

—**Gary Snyder,** "Blue Mountains Constantly Walking"

Human walking is a unique activity during which the body, step by step, teeters on the edge of catastrophe. . . . Man's bipedal mode of walking seems potentially catastrophic because only the rhythmic forward movement of first one leg and then the other keeps him from falling flat on his face.

—**John Napier,** "The Antiquity of Human Walking"

And did those feet in ancient time
Walk upon England's mountains green?
—**William Blake,** "And Did Those Feet"

***

The second day after Wordsworth came to me, dear Sara accidently emptied a skillet of boiling milk on my foot, which confined me during the whole of C. Lamb's stay & still prevents me from all *walks* longer than a furlong.
   —**Samuel Taylor Coleridge,** letter to Robert Southey

***

Trochee trips from long to short;
From long to long in solemn sort
Slow Spondee stalks; strong foot! yet ill able
Ever to come up with Dactyl trisyllable.
Iambics march from short to long;—
With a leap and a bound the swift Anapaests throng;
Amphibrachys hastes with a stately stride;—
First and last being long, middle short, Amphimacer

Strikes his thundering hoofs like a proud highbred
  Racer.
—**Samuel Taylor Coleridge,** "Metrical Feet. Lesson
  for a Boy"

Tender, too, is the silence of human feet. You have but to pass a season amongst the barefooted to find that man, who, shod, makes so much ado, is naturally as silent as snow. Woman, who not only makes her armed heel heard, but also goes rustling like a shower, is naturally silent as snow. The vintager is not heard among the vines, nor the harvester on his threshing-floor of stone. There is a kind of simple stealth in their coming and going, and they show sudden smiles and dark eyes in and out of the rows of harvest when you thought yourself alone. The lack of noise in their movement sets free the sound of their voices, and their laughter floats.
—**Alice Meynell,** "The Foot"

My foot is a border partaking of the double character of me and of the earth, a neutral zone separating me from the ground. . . . The footless, crippled beggars painted by Breughel are pathetic and disturbing chiefly because they have nothing between them and the earth. Without the foot do they qualify as human?

—**Richard M. Griffith,** "Anthropodology: Man A-Foot"

We begin our lives with such small,
such plump and perfect
infant feet, slivers of pink pearl for toenails,
it's laughable to think of their ever sustaining
The whole weight of a body.

—**Denise Levertov,** "Feet"

all my life
always on the go
keep on doing
the old heel and toe

put one in front
then put the other
same old way
I learnt from my mother

blister on my heel
don't know when I'll eat
same old business
walking on my feet

I know where I'm going
walking on my feet
reckon when I get there
I'll be dead beat
—**A. R. D. Fairburn,** "Walking on My Feet"

once I dreamt of a form of poetry created by the sound of
feet walking in the grass
—**Cecilia Vicuna,** "The Resurrection of the Grasses"

There they can switch their feet, and oh! the different
ways they're able to walk!
—**Elias Canetti,** *Notes from Hampstead*

The bridges are suspended as if a person walking
had no anchor in any world
and the foot lands after the foot
like a victim of amnesia in his brand new life.
—**Cole Swensen,** *Walk*

And all this Vegetable World appeared on my left Foot,
As a bright sandal formed immortal of precious stones &
gold:
I stooped down & bound it on to walk forward thro'
Eternity.
—**William Blake,** *Milton*

It looks as if
Iris flowers had bloomed
On my feet—
Sandals laced in blue.
—**Matsuo Bashō,** *The Narrow Road to the Deep North*

If it's chariots or sandals,
I'll take sandals.
—**Denise Levertov,** "A Traveler"

I belong to a family in which everyone has sound, solid shoes. My mother possessed so many pairs of shoes that she even had to have a little wardrobe made especially for them. Whenever I visit them they utter cries of indignation and sorrow at the sight of my shoes. But I know that it is possible to live even with worn-out shoes. During the German occupation I was alone here in Rome, and I only had one pair of shoes. If I had taken them to a cobbler's I would have had to stay in bed for two or three days, and in my situation that was impossible. So I continued to wear them and when—on top of everything else—it rained, I felt them gradually falling apart, becoming soft and shapeless, and I felt the coldness of the pavement beneath the soles of my feet. This is why I still wear worn-out shoes, because I remember that particular pair and compared with them my present shoes don't seem too bad; besides, if I have money I would rather spend it on something else as shoes don't seem to me to be very essential things.

—**Natalia Ginzburg,** "Worn-Out Shoes"

And now walk on. Oh, it is heavenly and good and in simplicity most ancient to walk on foot, provided of course one's shoes or boots are in order.

—**Robert Walser,** *The Walk*

Paths and Roads

A road is the site of many journeys. The place of a walk is there before the walk and after it.

—**Richard Long,** "Five Six Pick Up Sticks, Seven Eight Lay Them Straight"

People love bypaths.
—*Tao Te Ching*

❂

You cannot travel on the path before you have become the path itself.
—**Gautama Buddha**

❂

Socrates: Where do you come from, Phaedrus my friend, and where are you going?

Phaedrus: I've been with Lysias, Socrates, the son of Cephalus, and I'm off for a walk outside the wall, after a long morning's sitting there. On the instructions of our common friend Acumenus I take my walks on the open roads; he tells me that is more invigorating than walking in the colonnades.

Socrates: Yes, he's right in saying so.
—**Plato,** *Phaedrus*

❂

Jog on, jog on, the foot-path way,
And merrily hent the stile-a:
A merry heart goes all the day,
Your sad tires in a mile-a.
—**William Shakespeare,** *The Winter's Tale*

Yet still the little path winds on and on
Down hedgerow sides and many a pastoral charm;
We soon forget the charm of poesy gone
In the still woodland with its silent balm,
And find some other joy to dream upon. . . .
—**John Clare,** "Footpaths"

Haunts of my youth!
Scenes of fond day dreams, I behold ye yet!
Where 'twas so pleasant by thy northern slopes
To climb the winding sheep-path, aided oft
By scatter'd thorns: whose spiny branches bore
Small wooly tufts, spoils of the vagrant lamb
There seeking shelter from the noon-day sun;

And pleasant, seated on the short soft turf,
To look beneath upon the hollow way
While heavily upward mov'd the labouring wain,
And stalking slowly by, the sturdy hind
To ease his panting team, stopp'd with a stone
The grating wheel.
—**Charlotte Smith,** *Beachy Head*

What is it that makes it so hard sometimes to determine whither we will walk? . . . We would fain take that walk, never yet taken by us through this actual world, which is perfectly symbolical of the path which we love to travel in the interior and ideal world; and sometimes, no doubt, we find it difficult to choose our direction, because it does not yet exist distinctly in our idea.
—**Henry David Thoreau,** "Walking"

Florida is so watery and vine-tied that pathless wanderings are not easily possible in any direction. I started to cross the State by a gap hewn for the locomotive, walking some-

times between the rails, stepping from tie to tie, or walking
on the strip of sand at the sides, gazing into the mysterious
forest.

—**John Muir,** *A Thousand-Mile Walk to the Gulf*

When first I walked here I hobbled
along ties set too close together
for a boy to step naturally on each.
When I grew older, I thought, my stride
would reach every other and thereafter
I would walk in time with the way
toward the meeting place of rails
in that yellow Lobachevskian haze up ahead.

—**Galway Kinnell,** "The Seekonk Woods"

The green roads that end in the forest
Are strewn with white goose feathers this June,
Like marks left behind by someone gone to the forest
To show his track. But he has never come back.

—**Edward Thomas,** "The Green Roads"

The highway lengths of dust and stone
Lie grey in blinding heat,
For throbbing heads no shadow thrown,
No turf for weary feet.
I tempt the worn way-farer's tread—
Green portals arching wide,
Green grass below, green leaves o'erhead,
Green banks on either side.
—**Tom Taylor,** "The Green Lane"

There were several roads near by, but it did not take her long to find the one paved with yellow bricks. Within a short time she was walking briskly toward the Emerald City, her silver shoes tinkling merrily on the hard, yellow road-bed. The sun shone bright and the birds sang sweetly, and Dorothy did not feel nearly so bad as you might think a little girl would who had been suddenly whisked away from her own country and set down in the midst of a strange land.

—**L. Frank Baum,** *The Wonderful Wizard of Oz*

One fine winter's day when Piglet was brushing away the snow in front of his house, he happened to look up, and there was Winnie-the-Pooh. Pooh was walking round and round in a circle, thinking of something else, and when Piglet called to him, he just went on walking.

"Hallo!" said Piglet, "what are *you* doing?"

"Hunting," said Pooh.

"Hunting what?"

"Tracking something," said Winnie-the-Pooh very mysteriously.

"Tracking what?" said Piglet, coming closer.

"That's just what I ask myself. I ask myself, What?"

—**A. A. Milne**, *Winnie-the-Pooh*

But it is preeminently as the deepest layer of my mental soil, as the firm ground on which I still stand, that I regard the Méséglise and Guermantes ways. It is because I believed in things and in people while I walked along those paths that the things and the people they made known to me are the only ones that I still take seriously and that still bring me joy.

—**Marcel Proust**, *Swann's Way*

Summer was the passage through. I remember first the long stone path next to a meadow in Prospect Park where as a child I ran off one summer twilight just in time to see the lamplighter go from lamp to lamp touching each gas mantle with the upraised end of a pole so that it suddenly flamed. On the other side of those lamps, the long meadow was stormy-green and dark; but along the path, the flames at each lamp flared in yellow and green petals.

—**Alfred Kazin,** *A Walker in the City*

My walking is of two kinds: one straight on end to a definite goal at a round pace; one, objectless, loitering, and purely vagabond. In the latter state, no gypsy on earth is a greater vagabond than myself; it is so natural to me, and strong with me, that I think I must be the descendant, at no great distance, of some irreclaimable tramp.

—**Charles Dickens,** "Shy Neighborhoods"

I choose the road from here to there
When I've a scandalous tale to bear,
Tools to return or books to lend
To someone at the other end.

But I avoid it when I take
A walker's walk for walking's sake:[. . .]
No, when a fidget in the soul
Or cumulus clouds invite a stroll,
The route I pick goes roundabout
To finish where it started out.
—**W. H. Auden,** "Walks"

Labyrinths are usually in the form of a circle with a meandering but purposeful path, from the edge to the center and back out again. Each one has only one path, and once we make the choice to enter it, the path becomes a metaphor for our journey through life.
—**Lauren Artress,** *Walking a Sacred Path*

. . . on foot you soon learn how high is a hill and how long is a mile. And when you have walked the same road through all the seasons, you know how certain is change and how gradual.

—**Hal Borland,** "To Own the Streets and Fields"

An aging pilgrim on a
Darkening path walks through the
Fallen and falling leaves. . . .
—**Kenneth Rexroth,** *On Flower Wreath Hill*

Follow the ax cut path
narrower than your hips
through the labyrinth
of trees toppled years ago
in fire.
—**Marge Piercy,** "Sand Roads"

How many roads must a man walk down
Before you can call him a man?
—**Bob Dylan,** "Blowin' in the Wind"

I planned each charted course
Each careful step along the byway
And more, much more than this
I did it my way.
—**Paul Anka,** "My Way"

When I look skyward while walking, I walk unaware on
a curve towards the north.
—**Werner Herzog,** *Of Walking in Ice*

Travelers should be aware that paths leading nowhere
are also part of the trip.
—**Raul Ruiz**

Two roads diverged in a wood, and I—
I took the one less traveled by.
—**Robert Frost,** "The Road Not Taken"

Morning

every morning
    I stroll out into the fields,
        I believe in everything—
I believe in anything—
—**Mary Oliver,** "The Pinewoods"

So it was, on this First Morning, that each drowsing Ancestor felt the Sun's warmth pressing on his eyelids and felt his body giving birth to children. . . .

In the bottom of their hollows (now filling up with water), the Ancients shifted one leg, then another leg. They shook their shoulders and flexed their arms. They heaved their bodies upward through the mud. Their eyelids cracked open. They saw their children at play in the sunshine.

The mud fell from their thighs, like placenta from a baby. Then, like the baby's first cry, each Ancestor opened his mouth and called out, "I AM!" "I am—Snake . . . Cockatoo . . . Honey-ant . . . honeysuckle . . ." and this first "I am!," this primordial act of naming, was held, then and forever after, as the most secret and sacred couplet of the Ancestor's song.

Each of the Ancients (now basking in the sunlight) put his left foot forward and called out a second name. He put his right foot forward and called out a third name. He named the waterhole, the reedbeds, the gum trees—calling to right and left, calling all things into being and weaving their names into verses.

The Ancients sang their way all over the world. They sang the rivers and ranges, salt-pans and sand dunes. They hunted, ate, made love, danced, killed: wherever their tracks led they left a trail of music.

—**Bruce Chatwin,** *The Songlines*

The morning's fair; the lusty Sun
With ruddy cheek begins to run;
And early birds, that wing the skies,
Sweetly sing to see him rise.
I am resolved, this charming day,
In the open field to stray,
And have no roof above my head,
But that whereon the gods do tread.
—**John Dyer,** "The Country Walk"

It was, by this time, within an hour of noon, and although a dense vapor still enveloped the city they had left, as if the very breath of its busy people hung over their schemes of gain and profit and found greater attraction there than in the quiet region above, in the open country it was clear and fair. Occasionally, in some low spots they came upon patches of mist which the sun had not yet driven from their strongholds; but these were soon passed, and as they laboured up the hills beyond, it was pleasant to look down, and see how the sluggish mass rolled heavily off, before the cheering influence of day. A broad, fine, honest sun lighted up the green pastures and dimpled water, with the semblance of summer, while it left the travellers all the invigorating freshness of that early time of year. The ground seemed elastic under their feet; the sheep bells were music to their ears; and exhilarated by exercise, and stimulated by hope, they pushed onward with the strength of lions.

—**Charles Dickens,** *Nicholas Nickleby*

As Adam early in the morning,
Walking forth from the bower refresh'd with sleep,
Behold me where I pass, hear my voice, approach,
Touch me, touch the palm of your hand to my body as
    I pass,
Be not afraid of my body.

—**Walt Whitman,** "As Adam Early in the Morning"

Mon luth! Mon luth! Walked from Undercliff to Fort Montgomery yesterday, just failing of West Point. A good 42 miles. Up at four with the help of an alarm clock. Had breakfast at Schwarzwalds (sausage + buckwheats) and then started. The Fifth Avenue hotel was covered with a strange astral light + looked very much like Rousseau's painting of Fontainebleau. Managed to get across the river by seven and from that time until half-past six at night, I walked without stopping longer than a minute or two at a time. How clean + precise the lines of the world are early in the morning! The light is perfect—absolute—one sees the bark of trees high up on the hills, the seams of rocks, the color + compass of things. Seven, too, seems to be a fine hour for dogs. They were nosing about all along the first stretches of road. One or two were stretched out on porches dozing away comfortably, ideally at their ease. The sun blazes wonderfully then, too. The mere roofs are like pools of fire. From the Palisades, I looked down on the Hudson, which glimmered incessantly. In the distance, the Sound shot up a flare. There was a ship below me + I made note of the whole business in a sketch on a scrap of paper, which I copy. Will it help me remember the thing.

—**Wallace Stevens,** journal entry

"But was the dawn wonderful?" asked Helen.

With unforgettable sincerity he replied: "No." The word flew again like a pebble from the sling. Down toppled all that had seemed ignoble or literary in his talk, down toppled tiresome R. L. S. and the "love of the earth" and his silk top-hat. In the presence of these women Leonard had arrived, and he spoke with a flow, an exultation, that he had seldom known.

"The dawn was only grey, it was nothing to mention—"

"Just a grey evening turned upside down, I know."

"—and I was too tired to lift up my head to look at it, and so cold too. I'm glad I did it, and yet at the time it bored me more than I can say. And besides—you can believe me or not as you choose—I was very hungry. That dinner at Wimbledon—I meant it to last me all night like other dinners. I never thought that walking would make such a difference. Why, when you're walking you want, as it were, a breakfast and luncheon and tea during the night as well, and I'd nothing but a packet of Woodbines. Lord, did I feel bad! Looking back, it wasn't what you may call enjoyment. It was more a case of sticking to it. I did stick. I—I was determined. Oh, hang it all! what's the good—I mean, the good of living in a room for ever? There one goes on day after day, same old game, same up and down to town, until you forget there is any other game. You ought to see once in a while what's going on outside, if it's only nothing in particular after all."

—**E. M. Forster,** *Howard's End*

And I walked, I walked through the light air;
I moved with the morning.
—**Theodore Roethke,** "A Field of Light"

I walked in a timeless morning past a row of white cottages, almost expecting that an ancient man with a great beard and an hourglass and a scythe under his nightdressed arm might lean from a window and ask me the time. I would have told him: "Arise, old counter of the heartbeats of albatrosses, and wake the cavernous sleepers of the town to a dazzling new morning." I would have told him: "you unbelievable father of Eva and Dai Adam, come out, old chicken, and stir up the winter morning with your spoon of a scythe." I would have told him—I would have scampered like a scalded ghost, over the cliffs and down into the bilingual sea.

—**Dylan Thomas,** "Quite Early One Morning"

The morning woods were utterly new. A strong yellow light pooled beneath the trees; my shadow appeared and vanished on the path, since a third of the trees I walked under were still bare, a third spread a luminous haze wherever they grew, and another third blocked the sun with new, whole leaves. The snakes were out—I saw a bright, smashed one on the path—and the butterflies were vaulting and furling about; the phlox was at its peak, and even the evergreens looked greener, newly created and washed.

—**Annie Dillard,** *Pilgrim at Tinker Creek*

The traveler sleeps like a log until the small hours of the morning, when the cocks crow for the first time and the old man wakes him up by passing some blades of grass over his face.

"Hail Mary."

"Conceived without sin."

"Shall we go?"

"Sure."

The old man gets up and stretches. He folds the blanket carefully, loads it on the donkey and yawns.

"I always start after twelve o'clock, when the cock crows. It's better walking then, don't you think? The morning was made for walking and the night for sleeping, I always say."

"Yes, I think so too."

The night is still dark. It is cool and the walking is pleasant.

—**Camilo José Cela,** *Journey to the Alcarria*

The little churches wake up in the half light,
slowly the nuns come out & walk across the bridges.

—**Aldo Palazzeschi,** "Nuns Go Walking"

March 27th.—It is a dull, grey morning, with a dewy feeling in the air; fresh, but not windy; cool, but not cold, the very day for a person newly arrived from the heat, the glare, the noise, and the fever of London, to plunge into the remotest labyrinths of the country, and regain the repose of mind, the calmness of heart, which has been lost in that great Babel. I must go violeting—it is a necessity—and I must go alone; the sound of a voice, even my Lizzy's, the touch of Mayflower's head, even the bounding of her elastic foot, would disturb the serenity of feeling which I am trying to recover. I shall go quite alone, with my little basket, twisted like a beehive, which I love so well, because *she* gave it to me, and kept sacred to violets and to those whom I love; and I shall get out of the high road the moment I can. I would not like to meet any one just now, even of those whom I best like to meet.

—**Mary Russell Mitford,** "Violeting"

I rose early, wrote, and loitered down the sunny lane before breakfast. A lovely morning and I heard the first turtle dove trilling.

—**The Reverend Francis Kilvert,** *Diary*

Night

In these divine pleasures permitted to me of walks in the June night under moon and stars, I can put my life as a fact before me and stand aloof from its honor and shame.

—**Ralph Waldo Emerson,** *Journals*

Sweet bird, that shunn'st the noise of folly,
Most musical, most melancholy!
Thee, chauntress, oft the woods among
I woo, to hear thy even-song;
And missing thee, I walk unseen
On the dry smooth-shaven green,
To behold the wandering Moon
Riding near her highest noon,
Like one that had been led astray
Through the heav'ns' wide pathless way;
And oft, as if her head she bowed,
Stooping through a fleecy cloud.
Oft on a plat of rising ground,
I hear the far-off curfew sound,
Over some wide-watered shore,
Swinging slow with sullen roar. . . .
—**John Milton,** "Il Penseroso"

In the evening walked alone down to the Lake by the
side of Crow Park after sunset and saw the solemn colour-
ing of night draw on, the last gleam of sunshine fading
away on the hilltops, the deep serene of the asters, and the

long shadows of the mountains thrown across them, till they nearly touched the hithermost shore. At distance heard the murmur of many waterfalls not audible in the day-time. Wished for the moon, but she was dark to me and silent, hid in her vacant interlunar cave.

—**Thomas Gray,** "Journal in the Lakes"

The clock has just struck two, the expiring taper rises and sinks in the socket, the watchman forgets the hour in slumber, the laborious and the happy are at rest, and nothing wakes but meditation, guilt, revelrie, and despair. The drunkard once more fills the destroying bowl, the robber walks his midnight round, and the suicide lifts his guilty arm against his own sacred person.

Let me no longer waste the night over the page of antiquity, or the sallies of contemporary genius, but pursue the solitary walk, where vanity, ever changing, but a few hours past walked before me, where she kept up the pageant, and now, like a froward child, seems hushed with her own importunities.

—**Oliver Goldsmith,** "A City Night-Piece"

We resume our way, independent and alone; for we have no companion this time, except our never-to-be-forgotten and ethereal companion, the reader. A real arm within another's puts us out of the pale of walking that is to be made good. It is good already. A fellow-pedestrian is company—is the party you have left; you talk and laugh, and there is no longer anything to be contended with. But alone, and in bad weather, and with a long way to go, here is something for the temper and spirits to grapple with and turn to account; and accordingly we are booted and buttoned up, an umbrella over our heads, the rain pelting upon it, and the lamp-light shining in the gutters; "mudshine," as an artist of our acquaintance used to call it, with a gusto of reprobation. Now, walk cannot be well worse; and yet it shall be nothing if you meet it heartily. There is a pleasure in overcoming obstacles; mere action is something; imagination is more; and the spinning of the blood, and vivacity of the mental endeavour, act well upon one another, and gradually put you in a state of robust consciousness and triumph. Every time you set down your leg you have a respect for it. The umbrella is held in the hand like a roaring trophy.

—**Leigh Hunt,** "Walks Home by Night"

Some years ago, a temporary inability to sleep, referable to a distressing impression, caused me to walk about the streets all night, for a series of several nights. The disorder might have taken a long time to conquer, if it had been faintly experimented on in bed; but, it was soon defeated by the brisk treatment of getting up directly after lying down, and going out, and coming home tired at sunrise.

In the course of those nights, I finished my education in a fair amateur experience of houselessness. My principal object being to get through the night, the pursuit of it brought me into sympathetic relations with people who have no other object every night in the year.

—**Charles Dickens,** "Night Walks"

Last night the moon rose behind four distinct pine-tree tops in the distant woods and the night at ten was so bright that I walked abroad. But the sublime light of night is unsatisfying, provoking; it astonishes but explains not. Its charm floats, dances, disappears, comes and goes, but palls in five minutes after you have left the house. Come out of your warm, angular house, resounding with few voices, into the chill, grand, instantaneous night, with such a Presence as a full moon in the clouds, and you are struck with poetic wonder. In the instant you leave far behind all human relations, wife, mother and child, and live only with the savages—water, air, light, carbon, lime, and granite. I think of Kuhleborn. I become a moist, cold element. 'Nature grows over me.' Frogs pipe; waters far off tinkle; dry leaves hiss; grass bends and rustles, and I have died out of the human world and come to feel a strange, cold, aqueous, terraqueous, aerial, ethereal sympathy and existence. I sow the sun and moon for seeds.

—**Ralph Waldo Emerson,** *Journals*

I wander all night in my vision,
Stepping with light feet, swiftly and noiselessly stepping and stopping,
   Bending with open eyes over the shut eyes of sleepers,
   Wandering and confused, lost to myself, ill-assorted, contradictory,
   Pausing, gazing, bending, and stopping.
—**Walt Whitman,** "The Sleepers"

To know how to walk in the night, to have a goal, to reach it in the darkness, the shadows.

—**Joseph Joubert,** *Notebooks*

Thinking it over as we were walking with soft steps under the trees of the Champs-Elysees, I seemed to catch a purpose, that of all the night prowlers of Paris: we were in search of a corpse.

If all at once we had encountered a lifeless form lying prostrate on the pavement, bathed perhaps in his own blood, or propped against a wall, we should have come immediately to a halt and that night would have ended. But it was that encounter, and that encounter only, which could have satisfied us.

We know, that in Paris death alone has power to quench the pointless thirst, to bring to a close an aimless walk. A corpse confronts us with eternity.

O inviolable secret of Paris!

—**Philippe Soupault,** *Last Nights of Paris*

To walk in the night, to speak through din and confusion, so that the shaft of the rising day fuses and answers my step, designates the branch, and picks the fruit.

—**Jacques Dupin,** "I Am Forbidden . . . "

Twelve o'clock.
Along the reaches of the street
Held in a lunar synthesis,
Whispering lunar incantations
Dissolve the floors of memory
And all its clear relations
Its divisions and precisions,
Every street lamp that I pass
Beats like a fatalistic drum,
And through the spaces of the dark
Midnight shakes the memory
As a madman shakes a dead geranium.

—**T. S. Eliot,** "Rhapsody on a Windy Night"

I have been one acquainted with the night.
I have walked out in rain—and back in rain.
I have outwalked the furthest city light.
—**Robert Frost,** "Acquainted with the Night"

Coming up the subway stairs, I thought the moon
only another street-light—
a little crooked.
—**Charles Reznikoff,** *Walking and Watching*

who walked all night with their shoes full of blood on
the snowbank docks waiting for a door in the East River to
open to a room full of steamheat and opium
—**Allen Ginsberg,** "Howl"

When he had walked on the river's bank in the peaceful
moonlight for some half an hour, he put his hand in his
breast and tenderly took out the handful of roses. Perhaps

he put them to his heart, perhaps he put them to his lips, but certainly he bent down on the shore and gently launched them on the flowing river. Pale and unreal in the moonlight, the river floated them away.

—**Charles Dickens,** *Little Dorrit*

I go out walking after midnight
In the moonlight, just like we used to do
I'm always walking after midnight
Searching for you.

—**Patsy Cline,** "Walking after Midnight"

I wanted to die so I walked
the streets. Dead night,
black as iris, cold as the toes
on a barefoot drunk. Not a sound
but my shoes asking themselves over:
What season is this? Why is the wind
stuttering in its stall of nightmares?

—**Lorna Dee Cervantes,** "Colorado Blvd."

To enter out into that silence that was the city at eight o'clock of a misty evening in November, to put your feet upon that buckling concrete walk, to step over grassy seams and make your way, hands in pockets, through the silences, that was what Mr. Leonard Mead most dearly loved to do. He would stand upon the corner of an intersection and peer down long moonlit avenues of sidewalk in four directions, deciding which way to go, but it really made no difference; he was alone in this world of 2052 A.D., or as good as alone, and with a final decision made, a path selected, he would stride off, sending patterns of frosty air before him like the smoke of a cigar.

—**Ray Bradbury,** "The Pedestrian"

At dark yesterday I walked home through the golf course at the back of the campus. Enjoyed the marvelous alertness that comes with walking in the dark without a light. All the senses wake up. Hearing is more conscious and acute; peripheral vision becomes a necessary function; there is a complex, delicate *feeling* of the ground one is walking over. The body seems fill out to its limits with an intense consciousness of itself and of things around it. That was the first time I've walked in the dark that way, I think, since we left Kentucky.

—**Wendell Berry,** "Notes from an Absence
      and a Return"

Tonight I walk. I am watching the sky. I think of the people who came before me and how they knew the placement of stars in the sky, watched the moving sun long and hard enough to witness how a certain angle of light touched a stone only once a year. Without written records, they knew the gods of every night, the small, fine details of the world around them and of immensity above them.

Walking, I can almost hear the redwoods beating. And the oceans are above me here, rolling clouds, heavy and dark, considering snow. On the dry, red road, I pass the place of the sunflower, that dark and secret location where creation took place. I wonder if it will return this summer, if it will multiply and move up to the other stand of flowers in a territorial struggle.

—**Linda Hogan,** "Walking"

Sounds and Smells

The chorus-ending from Aristophanes, raised every night from every ditch that drains into the Mediterranean, hoarse and primeval as the raven's croak, is one of the grandest tunes to walk by. Or on a night in May, one can walk through the too rare Italian forests for an hour on end and never be out of hearing of the nightingale's song.

—**George Macaulay Trevelyan,** "Walking"

. . . brushing ankle-deep in flowers,
We heard behind the woodbine veil
The milk that bubbled in the pail,
And buzzings of the honied hour.

—**Alfred Lord Tennyson,** *In Memoriam: A. H. H.*

That constant pacing to and fro, that never-ending rest-
lessness, that incessant tread of feet wearing the rough stones
smooth and glossy—is it not a wonder how the dwellers in
narrow ways can bear to hear it! Think of a sick man in such
a place as Saint Martin's Court, listening to the footsteps,
and in the midst of pain and weariness obliged, despite himself (as though it were a task he must perform), to detect the
child's step from the man's, the slipshod beggar from the
booted exquisite, the lounging from the busy, the dull heel of
the sauntering outcast from the quick tread of an expectant
pleasure-seeker—think of the hum and noise being always
present to his senses, and of the stream of life that will not
stop, pouring on, on, on, through all his restless dreams, as if
he were condemned to lie dead but conscious, in a noisy
churchyard, and had no hope of rest for centuries to come.

—**Charles Dickens,** *The Old Curiosity Shop*

As I went along the street where I live, I was suddenly *gripped* by a rhythm which took possession of me and soon gave me the impression of some force outside myself. It was as though someone else were making use of my *living-machine*. Then another rhythm overtook and combined with the first, and certain strange *transverse* relations were set up between these two principles (I am explaining myself as best I can. They combined the movement of my walking legs and some kind of song I was murmuring, or rather which was being murmured *through me...*).

—**Paul Valéry,** "Poetry and Abstract Thought"

On these rocks, where there is no growth of vegetable or animal life, all the seasons are the same, and this June day is so full of autumn that I listen unconsciously for the rustle of dead leaves.

The first group of men are coming out of the chapel, followed by a crowd of women, who divide at the gate and troop off in different directions, while the men linger on the road to gossip. The silence is broken; I can hear far off, as if over water, a faint murmur of Gaelic.

—**J. M. Synge,** *The Aran Islands*

There are meadowlarks and quail in the open land. One day late in the afternoon I walked about among the headstones at Rainy Mountain Cemetery. The shadows were very long, there was a deep blush on the sky, and the dark red earth seemed to glow with the setting sun. For a few moments, at that particular time of the day, there is a deep silence. Nothing moves, and it does not occur to you to make any sound. Something is going on there in the shadows. Everything has slowed to a stop in order that the sun might take leave of the land. And then there is the sudden, piercing call of a bobwhite. The whole world is startled by it.

—**N. Scott Momaday,** *The Way to Rainy Mountain*

I walked away in that wine air, and climbed up alone into the silence of a hill above the village, and thence I looked down upon it. It lay like a bowl of sugar nobs in the hills. As the darkening fountains of the dusk sweetened the sky, the outside silence of the world tightened so that even the clip of an insect was a cry, and the clinking and noising of the village minute orchestrations. The air became aqueous with bells. There were the bells of the goats as they stepped down into the village, stout udders stiffly jerking, bells that twinkled music like stars in the streets. The creatures scattered with that air of learned inquiry into the Plaza, dispersed in the streets, wandered in and out of the cottages, and everywhere they went their watery, seeking bell-music sang, deep now, and then trilling as though every particle of the falling dusk was carillon and the first white stars clangouring bells above them. The world was melting into bells.

—V. S. Pritchett, *Marching Spain*

As I resumed my walk, the slow strokes of the axe began again. I was reminded of the huge clock that used to stand on our mantel shelf when I was a boy. If one noticed carefully, he could tell by the slowing up of the tick-tock when the clock needed rewinding. But no rewinding will accelerate the tick-tocking of these strokes I hear today in the quiet cedar brake.

—**Roy Bedicheck,** *Adventures of a Texas Naturalist*

The air was soft and grey and mild and evening was coming. There was the smell of evening in the air, the smell of the fields in the country where they digged up turnips to peel them and eat them when they went out for a walk to Major Barton's, the smell there was in the little wood beyond the pavilion where the gallnuts were.

—**James Joyce,** *A Portrait of the Artist as a Young Man*

Mrs. Todd was an ardent lover of herbs, both wild and tame, and the sea-breezes blew into the low end-window of the house laden with not only sweet-brier and sweet-mary, but balm and sage and borage and mint, wormwood and southernwood. If Mrs. Todd had occasion to step into the far corner of her herb plot, she trod heavily upon thyme, and made its fragrant presence known with all the rest. Being a very large person, her full skirts brushed and bent almost every slender stalk that her feet missed. You could always tell when she was stepping about there, even when you were half awake in the morning, and learned to know, in the course of a few weeks' experience, in exactly which corner of the garden she might be.

—**Sarah Orne Jewett,** *The Country of the Pointed Firs*

Usually, at that hour of the early evening when I passed through on my way to the new library, they were all still at supper. The streets were strangely empty except for an old man in a white cap who sat on the curb sucking at a twisted Italian cigar. I felt I was passing through a deserted town and knocking my head against each door to call the inhabitants out. It was a poor neighborhood, poor as ours. Yet all the houses and stores there, the very lettering of the signs AVVOCAATO FARMACIA LATTERIA tantalized me by their foreignness. Everything there looked smaller and sleepier than it did in Brownsville. There was a kind of mild, infinitely soothing smell of flour and cheese mildly rotting in the evening sun. Your could almost taste the cheese in the sweat you licked off your lips, could feel your whole body licking and tasting at the damp inner quietness that came out of the stores. The heat seemed to melt down every hard corner in sight.

—**Alfred Kazin,** *A Walker in the City*

The heat in the street was terrible: and the airlessness, the bustle and the plaster, scaffolding, bricks, and dust all about him, and that special Petersburg stench, so familiar to all who are unable to get out of town in summer—all worked painfully upon the young man's already over-wrought nerves. The insufferable stench from the pot-houses, which are particularly numerous in that part of the town, and the drunken men whom he met continually, although it was a working day, completed the revolting misery of the picture. An expression of the profoundest disgust gleamed for a moment in the young man's refined face. He was, by the way, exceptionally handsome, above the average in height, slim, well-built, with beautiful dark eyes and dark brown hair. Soon he sank into deep thought, or more accurately speaking into a complete blankness of mind; he walked along not observing what was about him and not caring to observe it. From time to time, he would mutter something, from the habit of talking to himself, to which he had just confessed. At these moments he would become conscious that his ideas were sometimes in a tangle and that he was very weak; for two days he had scarcely tasted food.

—**Fyodor Dostoyevsky,** *Crime and Punishment*

Woods, Fields, and Mountains

When we walk, we naturally go to the fields and woods: what would become of us, if we walked only in a garden or a mall?

—**Henry David Thoreau,** "Walking"

Now as for spring, my liking is so cast
That of all the meadow flowers in sight,
I most adore those flowers red and white
Which men call daisies in the region round.
To them I'm so affectionately bound,
As I declared before, in time of May,
That when I lie in bed there dawns no day
But has me up and walking on the lawn
To see these flowers spread towards the dawn
When sunrise brings the light with brilliant sheen,
The livelong day thus walking on the green.
—**Geoffrey Chaucer,** *The Legend of Good Women*

Sometime walking, not unseen,
By hedge-row elms, on hillocks green,
Right against the eastern gate,
Where the great sun begins his state,
Robed in flames, and amber light,
The clouds in thousand liveries dight;
While the ploughman near at hand
Whistles o'er the furrowed land,
And the milkmaid singeth blithe,

And the mower whets his scythe,
And every shepherd tells his tale
Under the hawthorn in the dale.
Straight mine eye hath caught new pleasures
Whilst the landscape round it measures;
Russet lawns, and fallows grey,
Where the nibbling flocks do stray;
Mountains, on whose barren breast
The lab'ring clouds do often rest;
Meadows trim with daisies pied,
Shallow brooks, and rivers wide.
Towers and battlements it sees
Bosomed high in tufted trees,
Where perhaps some Beauty lies,
The Cynosure of neighb'ring eyes.
—**John Milton,** "L'Allegro"

I nauseate walking; 'tis a country diversion, I loathe the
country.
—**William Congreve,** *The Way of the World*

Coming thro' the rye, poor body,
Coming thro' the rye,
She draiglet a' her petticoatie
Coming thro' the rye.
—**Robert Burns,** "Coming Through the Rye"

An early worshipper at Nature's shrine,
I loved her rudest scenes—warrens, and heaths,
And yellow commons, and birch-shaded hollows,
And hedge rows, bordering unfrequented lanes
Bowered with wild roses, and the clasping woodbine
Where purple tassels of the tangling vetch
With bittersweet, and bryony inweave,
And the dew fills the silver bindweed's cups—
I loved to trace the brooks whose humid banks
Nourish the harebell, and the freckled pagil;
And stroll among o'ershadowing woods of beech,
Lending in Summer, from the heats of noon
A whispering shade; while haply there reclines
Some pensive lover of uncultured flowers,
Who, from the tumps with bright green mosses clad,
Plucks the wood sorrel, with its light thin leaves,

Heart-shaped, and triply folded; and its root
Creeping like beaded coral; or who there
Gathers, the copse's pride, anemones,
With rays like golden studs on ivory laid
Most delicate; but touched with purple clouds,
Fit crown for April's fair but changeful brow.
—**Charlotte Smith,** *Beachy Head*

We had a delightful journey. At the beginning of the first Park William got upon the pony, and betwixt a walk and a run, I kept pace with him while he trotted to the next gate—then I mounted again. We were joined by two travellers, like ourselves, with one white horse between them. We went on in company till we came near to Patterdale, trotting all the time. The trees in Gowbarrow Park were very beautiful, the hawthorns leafless, their round heads covered with rich red berries, and adorned with arches of green brambles; and eglantine hung with glossy hips; many birches yet tricked out in full foliage of bright yellow; oaks brown or leafless; the smooth silver branches of the ashes bare; most of the alders green as in spring.
—**Dorothy Wordsworth,** "Excursion on the Banks
of Ullswater"

The ground was hard, the air was still, my road was lonely; I walked fast till I got warm, and then I walked slowly to enjoy and analyse the species of pleasure brooding for me in the hour and situation. It was three o'clock; the church bell tolled as I passed under the belfry: the charm of the hour lay in its approaching dimness, in the low-gliding and pale-beaming sun. I was a mile from Thornfield, in a lane noted for wild roses in summer, for nuts and blackberries in autumn, and even now possessing a few coral treasures in hips and haws, but whose best winter delight lay in its utter solitude and leafless repose. If a breath of air stirred, it made no sound here; for there was not a holly, not an evergreen to rustle, and the stripped hawthorn and hazel bushes were as still as the white, worn stones which causewayed the middle of the path. Far and wide, on each side, there were only fields, where no cattle now browsed; and the little brown birds, which stirred occasionally in the hedge, looked like single russet leaves that had forgotten to drop.

—**Charlotte Brontë,** *Jane Eyre*

It was the most delightful of all days for a walk, with a dash of invigorating ice-temper in the air, but a coolness that soon gave place to the brisk glow of exercise, while the vigor remained as elastic as before. The atmosphere had a spirit and sparkle in it. Each breath was like a sip of ethereal wine, tempered, as I said, with a crystal lump of ice. . . . The pathway of that walk still runs along, with sunny freshness, through memory. I know not why it should be so. But my mental eye can even now discern the September grass, bordering the pleasant roadside with a brighter verdure than while the summer-heats were scorching it; the trees, too, mostly green, although, here and there, a branch or shrub has donned its vesture of crimson and gold, a week or two before its fellows. I see the tufted barberry bushes with their small clusters of scarlet fruit; the toadstools, likewise, some spotlessly white, others yellow or red—mysterious growths, springing suddenly from no root or seed, and growing nobody can tell how or wherefore. In this respect, they resembled many of the emotions in my breast. And I still see the little rivulets, chill, clear, and bright, that murmured beneath the road, through subterranean rocks, and deepened into mossy pools where tiny fish were darting to-and-fro, and within which lurked the hermit-frog.

—**Nathaniel Hawthorne,** *The Blithedale Romance*

Crossing a bare common, in snow puddles, at twilight, under a clouded sky, without having in my thoughts any occurrence of special good fortune, I have enjoyed a perfect exhilaration. I am glad to the brink of fear. In the woods too, a man casts off his years, as the snake his slough, and at what period soever of life, is always a child. In the woods, is perpetual youth. Within these plantations of God, a decorum and sanctity reign, a perennial festival is dressed, and the guest sees not how he should tire of them in a thousand years. In the woods, we return to reason and faith. There I feel that nothing can befall me in life,—no disgrace, no calamity, (leaving me my eyes,) which nature cannot repair. Standing on the bare ground,—my head bathed by the blithe air, and uplifted into infinite space,—all mean egotism vanishes. I become a transparent eye-ball; I am nothing; I see all; the currents of the Universal Being circulate through me; I am part or particle of God. The name of the nearest friend sounds then foreign and accidental: to be brothers, to be acquaintances, —master or servant, is then a trifle and a disturbance. I am the lover of uncontained and immortal beauty. In the wilderness, I find something more dear and connate than in streets or villages. In the tranquil landscape, and especially in the distant line of the horizon, man beholds somewhat as beautiful as his own nature.   **—Ralph Waldo Emerson,** "Nature"

The sun sets on some retired meadow, where no house is visible, with all the glory and splendor that it lavishes on cities, and perchance as it has never set before—where there is but a solitary marsh hawk to have his wings gilded by it, or only a musquash looks out from his cabin, and there is some little black-veined brook in the midst of the marsh, just beginning to meander, winding slowly round a decaying stump. We walked in so pure and bright a light, gilding the withered grass and leaves, so softly and serenely bright, I thought I had never bathed in such a golden flood, without a ripple or a murmer to it. The west side of every wood and rising ground gleamed like the boundary of Elysium, and the sun on our backs seemed like a gentle herdsman driving us home at evening.

—**Henry David Thoreau,** "Walking"

A rapid walker poetically and humourously minded gathers multitudes of images on his way. And rain, the heaviest you can meet, is a lively companion when the resolute pacer scorns discomfort of wet clothes and squealing boots. South-western rain-clouds, too, are never long sullen; they enfold and will have the earth in a good strong glut of the kissing overflow; then, as a hawk with feathers on his beak of the bird in his claw lifts his head, they rise and take veiled feature in long climbing watery lines: at any moment they may break the veil and show soft upper cloud, show sun on it, show sky, green near the verge they spring from, of the green of grass in early dew; or, along a travelling steep that rolls asunder overhead, heaven's laughter of purest blue among titanic white shoulders: it may mean fair smiling for a while or be the lightest interlude; but the water lines, and the drifting, the chasing, the upsoaring, all in a shadowy fingering of form, and the animation of the leaves of the trees pointing them on, the bending of the tree-tops, the snapping of branches, and the hurrahings of the stubborn hedge at wrestle with the flaws, yielding but a leaf at most, and that on a fling, make a glory of contest and wildness without aid of colour to inflame the man who is at home in them from old association on road, heath, and mountain. Let him be drenched, his heart will sing.

—**George Meredith,** *The Egoist*

Surely all other leisure is hurry compared with a sunny walk through the fields from "afternoon church"—as such walks used to be in those old leisurely times, when the boat, gliding sleepily along the canal, was the newest locomotive wonder; when Sunday books had most of them old brown-leather covers, and opened with remarkable precision always in one place.

—**George Eliot,** *Adam Bede*

Spongy meads, that soughed under the feet and grew steeper as one rose, took up the first few hundred feet. Little rivulets of mere dampness ran in among the under moss, and such very small hidden flowers as there were drooped with the surfeit of moisture. The rain was now indistinguishable from a mist, and indeed I had come so near to the level belt of cloud, that already its gloom was exchanged for that diffused light which fills vapours from within and lends them their mystery. A belt of thick brushwood and low trees lay before me, clinging to the slope, and as I pushed with great difficulty and many turns to right and left through its tangle a wisp of cloud enveloped me, and from that time on I was now in, now out of a deceptive drifting fog. . . .

—**Hilaire Belloc,** "The Brienzer Grat"

. . . in walking, even in that poor way, when, on account of physical weakness, it was often a pain and weariness, there are alleviations which may be more to us than positive pleasures, and scenes to delight the eye that are missed by the wheelman in his haste, or but dimly seen or vaguely surmised in passing—green refreshing nooks and crystal streamlets, and shadowy woodland depths with glimpses of a blue sky beyond—all in the wilderness of the human heart.

—**W. H. Hudson,** *Afoot in England*

O why do you walk through the fields in gloves,
Missing so much and so much?
O fat white woman whom nobody loves,
Why do you walk through the fields in gloves
When the grass is soft as the breast of doves
And shivering-sweet to the touch?
—**Frances Cornford,** "To a Fat Lady Seen from
the Train"

I walked with a young dryad through the woods,
And though the town poured out its noisy folk
That all might seem as common as the street
Under the palace of leaves, yet nothing broke
The sweet antiquity wherein my feet
Kept pace with a young dryad through the woods.
—**A. E.,** "Platonies"

In the platinum forest walked a white maiden
—**Paul Bowles,** "Prelude and Dance"

Next day, after paying what I liked at the inn, and
promising the hostess that I would learn Welsh, I walked
for twenty miles over stony roads gleaming with rain upon
the white thorns and bloom on the sloes, and through
woods where nothing brooded solemnly over grey moss and
green moss on the untrodden, rotten wood, and up dry, lad-
der-like beds of brooks that served as paths, over peat and
brindled grass, and along golden hazel hedges, where grew
the last meadow-sweet with herb-robert and harebell and

one wild rose, and above little valleys of lichened ash trees; and sometimes beneath me, and sometimes high above, the yellow birches waved in the rain, like sunset clouds fettered to the ground and striving and caracoling in their fetters.

—**Edward Thomas,** *Wales*

I took a long walk north of the town, out into the pastures where the land was so rough that it had never been ploughed up, and the long red grass of early times still grew shaggy over the draws and hillocks. Out there I felt at home again. Overhead the sky was that indescribable blue of autumn; bright and shadowless, hard as enamel. To the south I could see the dun-shaded river bluffs that used to look so big to me, and all about stretched drying cornfields, of the pale-gold colour, I remembered so well. Russian thistles were blowing across the uplands and piling against the wire fences like barricades. Along the cattle-paths the plumes of goldenrod were already fading into sun-warmed velvet, grey with gold threads in it. . . . As I wandered over those rough pastures, I had the good luck to stumble upon a bit of the first road that went from Black Hawk out to the north country; to my grandfather's farm, then on to the

Shimerdas' and to the Norwegian settlement. Everywhere else it had been ploughed under when the highways were surveyed; this half-mile or so within the pasture fence was all that was left of that old raod which used to run like a wild thing across the open prairie, clinging to the high places and circling and doubling like a rabbit before the hounds.

—**Willa Cather,** *My Antonia*

Now and then there was a quivering in the thicket. Old Phoenix said, "Out of my way, all you foxes, owls, beetles, jack rabbits, coons and wild animals!. . . . Keep out from under these feet, little bob-whites. . . . Keep the big wild hogs out of my path. Don't let none of those come running my direction. I got a long way." Under her small black-freckled hand her cane, limber as a buggy whip, would switch at the brush as if to rouse up any hiding things.

On she went. The woods were deep and still. The sun made the pine needles almost too bright to look at, up where the wind rocked. The cones dropped as light as feathers. Down in the hollow was the mourning dove—it was not too late for him.

—**Eudora Welty,** "A Worn Path"

Then came a July day—around 1910, I suppose—when I felt the urge to explore the vast marshland beyond the Oredezh. After skirting the river for three or four miles, I found a rickety footbridge. While crossing over, I could see the huts of a hamlet on my left, apple trees, rows of tawny pine logs lying on a green bank, and the bright patches made on the turf by the scattered clothes of peasant girls, who, stark naked in shallow water, romped and yelled, heeding me as little as if I were the discarnate carrier of my present reminiscences.

—**Vladimir Nabokov,** *Speak, Memory*

I was forging along the crest of a ridge, finding a way between stocky deep red mature manzanita trunks, picking the route and heading briskly on. Crawling.

Not hiking or sauntering or strolling, but *crawling,* steady and determined, through the woods. We usually visualize an excursion into the wild as an exercise of walking upright. We imagine ourselves striding through open alpine terrain—or across the sublime space of a sagebrush basin—or through the somber understory of an ancient sugar-pine grove.

But it's not so easy to walk upright through the late-twentieth-century mid-elevation Sierra forests.
—**Gary Snyder,** "The Porous World"

My walks in the hills and hollows around my home have inevitably produced in my mind the awareness that I live in a diminished country. The country has been and is being reduced by the great centralizing process that is our national economy. As I walk, I am always reminded of the slow, patient building of soil in the woods. And I am reminded of the events and companions of my life—for my walks, after so long, are cultural events. But under the trees and in the fields I see also the gullies and scars, healed or healing or fresh, left by careless logging and bad farming. I see the crumbling stone walls and the wire fences that have been rusting out ever since the 1930s. In the returning woods growth of the hollows, I see the sagging and the fallen barns, the empty and ruining houses, the houseless chimneys and foundations. As I look at this evidence of human life poorly founded, played out, and gone, I try to recover some understanding, some vision, of what this country was at the beginning: the great oaks and beeches and hickories, walnuts and maples, lindens and ashes, tulip poplars, standing in beauty and dignity now unimaginable, the black soil of their making, also no longer imaginable, lying deep at their feet—an incalcuable birthright sold for money . . .

—**Wendell Berry,** "The Work of Local Culture"

He wandered trails
through steep ravines and canyons
zig-zagging to the summit
of Mount Yahiko—
what did he find? A few clouds
above a vast sea of pine.

—**Sam Hamill,** "In Ryokan Country"

Walking along, gaining altitude, we fall into biologist's talk, nothing personal, about the landscapes we pass through. The switchbacks on the trail lead us up and out of scrub oak and ponderosa pine into lodgepole pine and aspen, then spruces and firs, and finally toward a world of strange, gnarled trees the likes of which appear only rarely in the West. There, near the harshest, most demanding sites, grow the limber pines, and above them, among the signs of want and scarcity, nearly waterless, wind-blown into fantastic shapes, are the ultimate members of the stone pine family, the bristlecone pines. . . .

Drawing near these patriarchs, exhausted, gasping for breath to express our wonder, we burr our palms on the prickly, spiny cones, then balm our wounds with the flecks of resin dotting the bright blue-green needles, always in bunches of five. The rigor of the growing conditions commands attention, even respect. Casting down our packs, shedding our physical burdens, we clasp the ancient trunks to us, as if they could speak to us of times past, of hardships endured, or hope for a world yet unseen.

—**Tom Wolf,** "A New Walk Is a New Walk"

On winter afternoons Richard and I cross through the woods behind the farm he rents, cross the long pasture where the white horse remains distant (wild mustard coming in strong here, come spring), and slip into the farther country along the creek, like salmon. The days are overcast and wet. We go miles without speaking.

Richard hands me a black cottonwood leaf that covers both my hands, and goes on. I examine it, expertly. The detritus of the forest floor that clings to it; the patches of disintegration where the gossamer veinery is exposed, like steel rods uncovered in a roadbed.

Two snails, barely visible, small as pinheads, chew at the leaf. Snails at work, tearing the woods apart.

We cast about for the dogs. Gone ahead somewhere. In the creek flats the alder is thick as row corn, and the signs of beaver are everywhere. We come to a skidway where they have cut and hauled, moved this fodder down to the bank, then off to deep water to anchor it against the hard months.

And here, deep in the woods, we find a huge ash, big enough and straight enough to floor my house four times over. But we aren't beaver. Or we care too much for such secrets, and move on.

—**Barry Lopez,** "Trying the Land"

Out walking in the frozen swamp one gray day
I paused and said, "I will turn back from here.
No, I will go on farther-and we shall see."
—**Robert Frost,** "The Wood-Pile"

River, Sea, and Shore

I will look at the footprints
going in and out of the water
and dream up a small blue god to talk to.
—**Gerald Stern,** "Here I Am Walking"

Calm was the day, and through the trembling air
Sweet-breathing Zephyrus did softly play
A gentle spirit, that lightly did delay
Hot Titan's beams, which then did glisten fair;
When I (whom sullen care,
Through discontent of my long fruitless stay
In prince's court, and expectation vain
Of idle hopes, which still do fly away
Like empty shadows, did afflict my brain),
Walk'd forth to ease my pain
Along the shore of silver-streaming Thames;
Whose rutty bank, the which his river hems,
Was painted all with variable flowers,
And all the meads adorn'd with dainty gems
Fit to deck maidens' bowers,
And crown their paramours,
Against the bridal day, which is not long:
  Sweet Thames run softly, till I end my song.
—**Edmund Spenser,** "Prothalamion"

Let us walk where reeds are growing,
By the alders in the mead;

Where the crystal streams are flowing,
In whose waves the fishes feed. . . .

Do not dread us, timid fishes,
We have neither net nor hook;
Wanderers we, whose only wishes
Are to read in nature's book.
—**Charlotte Smith**, "A walk by the water"

There was a feeling of freshness and vigour in the very streets; and when I got free of the town, when my foot was on the sands and my face towards the broad, bright bay . . . no language can describe the effect of the deep, clear azure of the sky and ocean, the bright morning sunshine on the semi-circular barrier of craggy cliffs surmounted by green swelling hills, and on the smooth, wide sands, and the low rocks out at sea . . . looking, with their clothing of weeds and moss, like little grass-grown islands—and above all, on the brilliant, sparkling waves. And then, the unspeakable purity and freshness of the air! there was just enough heat to enhance the value of the breeze, and just enough wind to keep the whole sea in motion, to make the waves come bounding to the shore, foaming and sparkling, as if wild with glee. Nothing else was stirring—no living creature was visible besides myself. My footsteps were the first to press the firm, unbroken sands; —nothing before had trampled them since last night's flowing tide had obliterated the deepest marks of yesterday, and left it fair and even, except where the subsiding water had left behind it the traces of dimpled pools, and little running streams.

—**Anne Brontë,** *Agnes Grey*

A tranquil summer sunset shone upon him as he approached the end of his walk, and passed through the meadows by the river side. He had that sense of peace, and of being lightened of a weight of care, which country quiet awakens in the breasts of dwellers in towns. Everything within his view was lovely and placid. The rich foliage of the trees, the luxuriant grass diversified with wild flower, the little green islands in the river, the beds of rushes, the water-lilies floating on the surface of the stream, the distant voices in boats borne musically towards him on the ripple of the water and the evening air, were all expressive of rest. In the occasional leap of a fish, or dip of an oar, or twittering of a bird not yet at roost, or distant barking of a dog, or lowing of a cow—in all such sounds, there was the prevailing breath of rest, which seemed to encompass him in every scent that sweetened the fragrant air. The long lines of red and gold in the sky, and the glorious track of the descending sun, were all divinely calm. Upon the purple tree-tops far away, and on the green height near at hand up which the shades were slowly creeping, there was an equal hush. Between the real landscape and its shadow in the water, there was no division; both were so untroubled and clear, and, while so fraught with solemn mystery of life and death, so hopefully reassuring to the gazer's soothed heart, because so tenderly and mercifully beautiful.

—**Charles Dickens,** *Little Dorrit*

Highways and cross-paths are hastily traversed; and, clambering down a crag, I find myself at the extremity of a long beach. How gladly does the spirit leap forth, and suddenly enlarge its sense of being to the full extent of the broad, blue, sunny deep! A greeting and a homage to the Sea! I descend over its margin, and dip my hand into the wave that meets me, and bathe my brow. That far-resounding roar is Ocean's voice of welcome. His salt breath brings a blessing along with it. Now let us pace together—the reader's fancy arm in arm with mine—this noble beach. which extends a mile or more from that craggy promontory to yonder rampart of broken rocks. In front, the sea; in the rear, a precipitous bank, the grassy verge of which is breaking away, year after year, and flings down its tufts of verdure upon the barrenness below. The beach itself is a broad space of sand, brown and sparkling, with hardly any pebbles intermixed. Near the water's edge there is a wet margin, which glistens brightly in the sunshine, and reflects objects like a mirror; and as we tread along the glistening border, a dry spot flashes around each footstep, but grows moist again, as we lift our feet. In some spots, the sand receives a complete impression of the sole—square toe and all; elsewhere, it is of such marble firmness, that we must stamp heavily to leave a print even of the iron-shod heel. Along the whole of this extensive beach gambols the surf-wave; now it makes a feint of dashing onward in a fury, yet dies away with a meek murmur, and does but kiss the strand; now, after many such abortive efforts, it rears itself up in an unbroken line, heightening as it advances, without a speck of foam on its green crest. With how fierce a roar it flings itself forward, and rushes far up the beach!

—**Nathaniel Hawthorne,** "Foot-prints on the Sea-shore"

As I ebb'd with the ocean of life,
As I wended the shores I know,
As I walk'd where the ripples continually wash you
      Paumanok,
Where they rustle up hoarse and sibilant,
Where the fierce old mother endlessly cries for her
      castaways,
I musing late in the autumn day, gazing off southward,
Held by this electric self out of the pride of which I utter
      poems,
Was seiz'd by the spirit that trails in the lines underfoot,
The rim, the sediment that stands for all the water and
      all the land of the globe.
—**Walt Whitman,** "As I Ebb'd with the Ocean of Life"

Walked from Point Lookout (which I reached by trolley and train and boat from Mineola) on the South Shore to Long Beach to-day: a very short walk perfect in itself but contemptible to get to and to come away from. I am not at home by the sea; my fancy is not at all marine, so to speak; when I sit on the shore and listen to the waves they only suggest wind in treetops. A single coup d'oeil is enough to see all, as a rule. The sea is loveliest far in the abstract when the imagination can feed upon the idea of it. The thing itself is dirty, wobbly and wet. But to-day, while all that I have just said was as true as ever, towards evening I saw lights on heaven and earth that never were seen before. The white beach (covered with beach-fleas etc.) ran along behind and before me. The declining sun threw my shadow a frightful length on the sand. The clouds began to become confused and dissolve into a golden mist into which the sea ran purple, blue, violet. The sun went down lighting the underworld and gilding a few clouds in this one. The West filled with a blue city of mist etc. Turning to the East I saw that a storm was creeping up, and suddenly then I caught sight of two rainbows swinging down. Walking over the beach under this lowering sky was like stepping into a cavern. Two women—one dressed in yellow, one in purple moving along the white sand—relieved the severity of the prospect.

—**Wallace Stevens,** journal entry

Stephen closed his eyes to hear his boots crush crackling wrack and shells. You are walking through it howsomever. I am, a stride at a time. A very short space of time through very short times of space. Five, six: the *nacheinander*. Exactly: and that is the ineluctable modality of the audible. Open your eyes. No. Jesus! If I fell over a cliff that beetles o'er his base, fell through the *nebeinander* ineluctably. I am getting on nicely in the dark. My ash sword hangs at my side. Tap with it: they do. My two feet in his boots are at the end of my legs, *nebeinander*. Sounds solid: made by the mallet of *Los Demiurgos*. Am I walking into eternity along Sandymount strand? Crush, crack, crik, crick. Wild sea money. Dominie Deasy kens them a'.

Won't you come to Sandymount,
Madeline the mare?

Rhythm begins, you see. I hear. A catalectic tetrameter of iambs marching. No, agallop: *deline the mare.*

Open your eyes now. I will. One moment. Has all vanished since? If I open and am for ever in the black adiaphane. *Basta!* I will see if I can see.

See now. There all the time without you: and ever shall be, world without end.

—**James Joyce,** *Ulysses*

We talked no more but walked on in the sunshine. I saw a ploughman hitching a black mule and a white mule together to plough down the weeds of a lot (they burn weeds in the spring as in the east we burn leaves in autumn); a schoolboy tying a paper streamer to a streetcar to watch the streamer curving in the wind; the lady of a house snapping up dandelions from her lawn and throwing them into the gutter (when I was a child we used to admire them); and a young woman in white trousers and a magenta shirt, her black curly hair carefully combed, walking slowly down the street. And all the while, to our right, we could see the surging waves and hear the squealing gulls.

—**Charles Reznikoff,** *The Manner Music*

I went for a walk over the dunes again this morning
to the sea,
then turned right along
  the surf
      rounded a naked headland
      and returned
  along the inland shore.
—**A. R. Ammons,** "Corsons Inlet"

City Walking

What oddities one finds in big cities when one knows how to roam and to look! Life swarms with innocent monsters.

—**Charles Baudelaire,** *Paris Spleen*

Every so often, I am walking through the streets, my eyes wide open, and I see—lots of ludicrous, even abominable things, and eventually something beautiful. I walk through the long, crooked, narrow streets redolent with the smell of a thousand disgusting fumes, along the narrow but high houses . . . almost as if to multiply the location. I twist myself through heaps of humans, screaming, running, panting, pushing each other, hitting, and turning around without complaining, I look at someone, he looks back . . . and we will both have forgotten about each other before we turn the corner.

—**Heinrich von Kleist,** letter

At this time appeared the type of the flaneur, who sauntered along aimlessly and covered the nothingness he detected around him and in him with innumerable impressions. Shop window displays, lithographs, new buildings, elegant attires, fancy coaches, newspaper vendors—indiscriminately he inhaled the images which pressed in upon him.

—**Siegfried Kracauer,** *The Mass Ornament*

Flanerie is a way of reading the street, in which people's faces, displays, shop windows, café terraces, cars, trucks, trees turn into an entire series of equivalent letters, which together form words, sentences, and pages of a book that is always new. In order to really stroll, one should not have anything too specific on one's mind.

—**Franz Hessel,** *Ein Flaneur in Berlin*

. . . I am a confirmed saunterer. I love to be set down haphazard among unknown byways; to saunter with open eyes, watching the moods and humors of men, the shapes of their dwellings, the criss-cross of their streets. It is an implanted passion that grows keener and keener. The everlasting lure of round-the-corner, how fascinating it is!

—**Christopher Morley,** "Sauntering"

But when the door shuts on us, all that vanishes. The shell-like covering which our souls have excreted to house themselves, to make for themselves a shape distinct from others, is broken, and there is left of all these wrinkles and roughnesses a central oyster of perceptiveness, an enormous eye. How beautiful a street is in winter! It is at once revealed and obscured. Here vaguely one can trace symmetrical straight avenues of doors and windows; here under the lamps are floating islands of pale light through which pass quickly bright men and women, who, for all their poverty and shabbiness, wear a certain look of unreality, an air of triumph, as if they had given life the slip, so that life, deceived of her prey, blunders on without them. But, after all, we are only gliding smoothly on the surface. The eye is not a miner, not a diver, not a seeker after buried treasure. It floats us smoothly down a stream; resting, pausing, the brain sleeps perhaps as it looks.

—**Virginia Woolf,** "Street Haunting"

In one of the streets I passed along on my endless wanderings I was surprised, many years earlier, by the first stirring of my sexual urge, under the oddest circumstances. It was on the Jewish New Year's Day, and my parents had made arrangements for me to attend some divine celebration. Probably, it was a service at the reformed synagogue, which my mother, on grounds of a family tradition, held in some sympathy, whereas my father's upbringing inclined him more to the orthodox rite. However, he had to give way. For this visit to the synagogue I had been entrusted to a relative whom I had to fetch on my way. But whether because I had forgotten his address or because I was unfamiliar with the district, it grew later and later without my drawing nearer to my goal. To make my way independently to the synagogue was out of the question, since I had no idea where it was. This bewilderment, forgetfulness, and embarrassment were doubtless due to my dislike of the impending service, in its familial no less than its divine aspect. While I was wandering thus, I was suddenly and simultaneously overcome, on the one hand, by the thought "Too late, time was up long ago, you'll never get there"—and, on the other, by a sense of the insignificance of all this, of the benefits of letting things take what course they would; and these two streams of consciousness converged irresistibly in an immense pleasure that filled me with blasphemous indifference toward the service, but exalted the street in which I stood as if it had already intimated to me the service of procurement it was later to render to my awakened drive.

—**Walter Benjamin,** "A Berlin Chronicle"

Even when I walk to the office in the morning I fancy I have achieved something more abiding than mere physical exercise. The first two blocks take me to the subway entrance. It's as soon as I have passed that, and have thus voluntarily chosen thirty minutes of walking instead of ten minutes of noisy riding, I feel myself reclaimed from civil activity. From that sense of civil freedom, to the Nirvana of vagrancy the path is straight and broad. In taking the first step I have done all that is really essential; I have lost identity in the city, and no one can tell what adventures lie ahead.

—**J. Brooks Atkinson,** Introduction to
Trevelyan's "Walking"

A city sidewalk by itself is nothing. It is an abstraction. . . . The same might be said of streets.

—**Jane Jacobs,** *The Death and Life of*
Great American Cities

You streets I take to pass some time of day
Or nighttime in the neutral open air!

Times when the rented room for which I pay
As if it could resent my mind's despair
Becomes like a trained nurse's torpid stare
Watching dead-eyed her feeble patient's malice—
When white walls feel like that, I leave the house.
Then, as dead poets did to ease their pain,
The pang of conscious love that grips the chest,
As those men wandered to a wood grown green
And seeing a day turn grew less depressed—
Who long are dead and their woods too are dead—
Like them I walk, but now walk streets instead.
—**Edwin Denby,** "Elegy—the Streets"

Every urban transportation plan should . . . put the pedestrian at the center of all its proposals, if only to facilitate wheeled traffic. But to bring the pedestrian back in to the picture, one must treat him with the respect and honor we now accord only to the automobile: we should provide him with pleasant walks, insulated from traffic, to take him to his destination, once he enters a business precinct or residential quarter. Every city should heed the example of Rotterdam in creating the Lignbaan, or of Coventry in creating its new shopping area. It is nonsense to say that this cannot be done in America, because no one wants to walk.

—**Lewis Mumford,** *The Highway and the City*

There are few greater delights than to walk up and down them in the evening alone with thousands of other people, up and down, relishing the lights coming through the trees or shining from the facades, listening to the sounds of music and foreign voices and traffic, enjoying the smell of flowers and good food and the air from the nearby sea. The sidewalks are lined with small shops, bars, stalls, dance halls, movies, booths lighted by acetylene lamps, and everywhere are strange faces, strange costumes, strange and delightful impressions. To walk up such a street into the quieter, more formal part of town, is to be part of a procession, part of a ceaseless ceremony of being initiated into the city and rededicating the city itself.

—**J. B. Jackson,** "The Stranger's Path"

Perception of the new qualities of the modern city had been associated, from the beginning, with a man walking,

as if alone, in its streets.
—**Raymond Williams**, *The Country and the City*

It's true, pedestrians really do
Slow things up—and this is a town
that hates to wait more than anything.
—**Ed Dorn**, "A Dispatch from the Front"

The ordinary practitioners of the city live "down below," below the thresholds at which visibility begins. They walk—an elementary form of this experience of the city; they are walkers, *Wandersmänner*, whose bodies follow the thicks and thins of an urban "text" they write without being able to read it. These practitioners make use of spaces that cannot be seen; their knowledge of them is as blind as that of lovers in each other's arms. The paths that correspond in this intertwining, unrecognized poems in which each body is an element signed by many others, elude legibility.
—**Michel de Certeau**, "Walking in the City"

❁

LONDON

When I am in a serious Humour, I very often walk by myself in Westminster Abbey; where the Gloominess of the Place, and the Use to which it is applied . . . are apt to fill the Mind with a kind of Melancholy, or rather Thoughtfulness, that is not disagreeable.

—**Joseph Addison,** *The Spectator*

❁

Where the fair columns of St. Clement stand,
Whose straiten'd bounds encroach upon the Strand;
Where the low penthouse bows the walker's head,
And the rough pavement wounds the yielding tread;
Where not a post protects the narrow space,
And strung in twines, combs dangle in thy face;
Summon at once thy courage, rouze thy care,
Stand firm, look back, be resolute, beware.

—**John Gay,** *Trivia; Or, The Art of Walking the Streets of London*

There is not a secret so aiding to the progress of sociality, as to get master of this short hand, and be quick in rendering the several turns of looks and limbs, with all their inflections and delineations, into plain words. For my own part, by long habitude, I do it so mechanically, that when I walk the streets of London, I go translating all the way; and have more than once stood behind in the circle, where not three words have been said, and have brought off twenty different dialogues with me, which I could have fairly wrote down and sworn to.

—**Laurence Sterne,** *A Sentimental Education*

I wander thro' each charter'd street,
Near where the charter'd Thames does flow,
And mark in every face I meet
Marks of weakness, marks of woe.
—**William Blake,** "London"

Being myself at that time, of necessity, a peripatetic, or walker of the streets, I naturally fell in more frequently with those female peripatetics who are technically called street-walkers. Many of these women had occasionally taken my part against watchmen who wished to drive me off the steps of houses where I was sitting.

——**Thomas De Quincey,** *Confessions of an English Opium Eater*

As I walked out one evening,
   Walking down Bristol Street,
The crowds upon the pavement
   Were fields of harvest wheat.
——**W. H. Auden,** "As I Walked Out One Evening"

PARIS

In Paris a stranger feels at home because he can inhabit the city the way he lives in his own four walls. And just as one inhabits an apartment, and makes it comfortable, by living in it instead of just using it for sleeping, eating, and working, so one inhabits a city by strolling through it without aim or purpose, with one's stay secured by the countless cafés which line the streets and past which the life of the city, the flow of pedestrians moves along.

—**Hannah Arendt,** Introduction to *Illuminations*

In a charming sally, Mme de Girardin one day said that for the Parisian, walking is not taking exercise—it is searching. . . . The Parisian truly seems an explorer, always ready to set off again, or, better, like some marvelous alchemist of life.

—**F. Bloch,** *Types du Boulevard*

Now you walk in Paris alone among the crowd
Herds of bellowing buses hemming you about
Anguish of love parching you within
As though you were never to be loved again
—**Guillaume Apollinaire,** "Zone"

Georgette resumed her stroll about Paris, through the mazes of the night. She went on, dispelling sorrow, solitude or tribulation. Then more than ever did she display her strange power: that of transfiguring the night. Thanks to her, who was no more than one of the hundred thousands, the Parisian night became a mysterious domain, a great and marvelous country, full of flowers, of birds, of glances and of stars, a hope launched into space. . . .

—**Philippe Soupault,** *Last Nights of Paris*

At the end of one afternoon, last year, in the side aisles of the "Electric-Palace," a naked woman, who must have come in wearing only a coat, strolled, dead white, from one row to the next.

—**André Breton,** *Nadja*

We passed by the pharmacy
                        Its flasks were day and night
Someone was brought in wounded
And in the crowd there was a woman singing
—**André Breton, Rene Char, Paul Eluard**, "A Walk"

✲

It seems it had been years but (she was remembering: a cold gray wind and the leaves went stuttering along the walls of the rue Clovis) it was hard keeping the cobble-stones silent as into the rue Descartes; a man (waving a green pantaloon before the auto bus) flattening into arm in arm. . . .

After that it had been easy and (she remembering) the rue Lacepede the rue (feeling smotheringly the smooth slipping of silk along the cool flesh of her thighs) Gracieuse the rue du Puits-de-l'Ermite (remembering) walking.

—**Robert M. Coates,** *The Eater of Darkness*

✲

NEW YORK

City of orgies, walks and joys,
City whom that I have lived and sung in your midst will
    one day make you illustrious,
Not the pageants of you, not your shifting tableaus, your
    spectacles, repay me,

Not the interminable rows of your houses, nor the ships at
    the wharves,
Nor the processions in the streets, nor the bright windows
    with goods in them,
Nor to converse with learn'd persons, or bear my share in
    the soiree or feast;
Not those, but as I pass O Manhattan, your frequent and
    swift flash of eyes offering me love,
Offering response to my own—these repay me,
Lovers, continual lovers, only repay me.
    —**Walt Whitman,** "City of Orgies"

The street curves in and out, up and down
in great waves of asphalt;
at night the granite tomb is noisy with starlings
like the creaking of many axles;
only the tired walker knows how much there is to climb,
how the sidewalk curves into the cold wind.
    —**Charles Reznikoff,** *Walking and Watching*

Leaving the Doubleday Bookstore, on 5th Ave

a few men and women in white tunics dancing on the side-
     walk

and the young men with shaved heads (in white) look like
     Trappist

novices,

　In a shop window:

　Mink. A Persian Lamb Leather Jacket.

　A brooch of diamonds and rubies . . .

A young fellow with a campaign button on his chest:
     IMPEACH
     NIXON

　Plastic women.

I cross the street in fear: WALK—DON'T WALK (in red)

　—**Ernesto Cardenal,** "Trip to New York"

I once started out

to walk around the world

but ended up in Brooklyn.

That Bridge was too much for me.

　　—**Lawrence Ferlinghetti,** "Autobiography"

I wanted to take a walk
and think of the city
whose only remaining beauty
is that you wrote about it.
—**Diane Wakoski,** "Walking Past Paul Blackburn's
Apt. on 7th St."

walking down park
amsterdam
or columbus do you ever stop
to think what it looked like
before it was an avenue
did you ever stop to think
what you walked
before you rode
subways to the stock
exchange (we can't be on
the stock exchange
we are the stock
exchanged)
—**Nikki Giovanni,** "Walking Down Park"

I'm becoming
the street.
 Who are you in love with?
me?
 Straight against the light I cross.
—**Frank O'Hara**, "Walking to Work"

OTHER CITIES

I think there can be nothing more delightful than a daily walk over the Capitol to visit the ruins of the Forum. In ancient times the Forum was to the city what the soul is to the body—the place in which is concentred all the most powerful and the best.—In the evening I go there again with Shelley—and see it under the grey eye of evening.
—**Claire Clairmont,** *Journals*

It has been observed that pedestrians here walk in "zigzags." This is simply on the overcrowding of the narrow sidewalks; nowhere else, except here and there in Naples, do you find sidewalks this narrow. This gives Moscow a provincial air, or rather the character of an improvised metropolis that has fallen into place overnight.

—**Walter Benjamin,** *Moscow Diary*

In order to feel at home in a strange city you need to have a secluded room to which you have a certain title and in which you can be alone when the tumult of new and incomprehensible voices becomes too great. The room should be quiet; no one should see you make your escape there, no one see you leave. The best thing is when you can slip into a cul-de-sac, stop at a door to which you have the key in your pocket, and unlock it without a soul hearing. . . .

You walk up and down and breathe in the silence. What has become of the atrocious bustle? The harsh light and the harsh sounds? The hundreds upon hundreds of faces? Few windows in these houses look onto the street, sometimes none at all; everything opens onto the courtyard, and this lies open to the sky. Only through the courtyard do you retain a mellow, tempered link with the world around you.

But you can also go up on the roof and see all the flat

roofs of the city at once. The impression is one of levelness, of everything being built in a series of broad terraces. You feel you could walk all over the city up there. The narrow streets present no obstacle; you cannot see them, you forget that there are streets.

—**Elias Canetti,** *The Voices of Marrakesh*

Thinking and Imagination

I can only meditate when I am walking. When I stop, I cease to think; my mind only works with my legs.

—**Jean-Jacques Rousseau,** *Confessions*

To *walk* abroad is, not with eyes,
But thoughts, the fields to see and prize;
Else may the silent feet,
Like logs of wood,
Move up and down, and see no good,
Nor joy nor glory meet.
—**Thomas Traherne,** "Walking"

A French author has advanced this seeming paradox, that *very few men know how to take a walk;* and, indeed, it is true, that few know how to take a walk with a prospect of any other pleasure, than the same company would have afforded them at home.

There are animals that borrow their colour from the neighbouring body, and, consequently, vary their hue as they happen to change their place. In like manner it ought to be the endeavour of every man to derive his reflections from the objects about him; for it is to no purpose that he alters his position, if his attention continues fixed to the same point.

—**Samuel Johnson,** *The Rambler*

Sweet pliability of man's spirit, that can at once surrender itself to illusions, which cheat expectation and sorrow of their weary moments!—long—long since had ye numbered out my days, had I not trod so great a part of them upon this enchanted ground. When my way is too rough for my feet, or too steep for my strength, I get off it, to some smooth velvet path which fancy has scattered over with rose-buds of delights; and having taken a few turns in it, come back strengthened and refreshed. . . .

—**Laurence Sterne,** *A Sentimental Education*

The leisurely moments of my daily walks have often been filled with charming periods of contemplation which I regret having forgotten. I will set down in writing those which still come to me and each time I reread them I will enjoy them anew. I will forget my misfortunes, my persecutors, my disgrace, while dreaming of the prize my heart deserved. These pages will, properly speaking, be only a shapeless diary of my reveries. There will be much concerning me in them, because a solitary person who reflects is necessarily greatly preoccupied with himself. Moreover, all the foreign ideas which pass through my head while I am walking will also find their place in them. I will say what I have thought just as it came to me and with as little connection as the ideas of the day before ordinarily have with those of the following day. But a new understanding of my natural temperament will come from . . . the daily fodder of my mind in the strange state I am in.

 —**Jean Jacques Rousseau,** *The Reveries of a*
Solitary Walker

Give me the clear blue sky over my head, and the green turf beneath my feet, a winding road before me, and a three hours' march to dinner—and then to thinking!

 —**William Hazlitt,** "On Going a Journey"

In one respect, at least, said I, after quitting the public road, in order to pursue a path, faintly tracked through the luxuriant herbage of the fields, and which left me at liberty to indulge the solitary reveries of a mind, to which the volume of nature is ever open at some page of instruction and delight;—in one respect, at least, I may boast of a resemblance to the simplicity of the ancient sages: I pursue my meditations on foot, and can find occasion for philosophic reflections, wherever yon fretted vault (the philosopher's best canopy) extends its glorious covering.

—**John Thelwall,** *The Peripatetic*

To rove about, musing, that is to say loitering, is, for a philosopher, a good way of spending time, especially in that kind of mock rurality, ugly but odd, and partaking of two natures, which surrounds certain large cities, particularly Paris.

—**Victor Hugo,** *Les Misérables*

At length, as we plodded along the dusty roads, our thoughts became as dusty as they; all thought indeed stopped, thinking broke down, or proceeded only passively in a sort of rhythmical cadence of the confused material of thought, and we found ourselves mechanically repeating some familiar measure which timed with our tread.

—**Henry David Thoreau,** "A Walk to Wachusett"

"One can only think or write while sitting" (Gustave Flaubert). Here I have got you, you nihilist! A sedentary life is the real sin against the Holy Spirit. Only those thoughts that come by walking have any value.

—**Friedrich Nietzsche,** *The Twilight of the Idols*

Walking is the natural recreation for a man who desires not absolutely to suppress his intellect but to turn it out to play for a season.

—**Leslie Stephen,** "In Praise of Walking"

The whole thing is planned on the model of an imaginary walk. First comes the dark wood of the authorities (who cannot see the trees), where there is no clear view and it is very easy to go astray. Then there is a cavernous defile through which I lead my readers—my specimens with its peculiarities, its details, its indiscretions, and its bad jokes—and then, all at once, the high ground and the prospect, and the question: "Which way do you want to go?"

—**Sigmund Freud,** letter to Wilhelm Fliess on
The Interpretation of Dreams

Perhaps
The truth depends on a walk around a lake,

A composing as the body tires, a stop
To see hepatica, a stop to watch
A definition growing certain and

A wait within that certainty, a rest
In the swags of pine-trees bordering the lake.
—**Wallace Stevens,** "Notes Toward a Supreme Fiction"

But what could be more absurd? It is, in fact, on the stroke of six; it is a winter's evening; we are walking to the Strand to buy a pencil. How then are we also on a balcony, wearing pearls in June? What could be more absurd? Yet it is nature's folly, not ours. When she set about her chief masterpiece, the making of man, she should have thought of one thing only. Instead, turning her head, looking over her shoulder, into each one of us she let creep instincts and desires which are utterly at variance with his main being, so that we are streaked, variegated, all of a mixture; the colors have run.
—**Virginia Woolf,** "Street Haunting"

Every thought sounds like a footfall,
Till a thought like a boot kicks down the wall.
—**Laura Riding,** "Footfalling"

Walks. The body advances, while the mind flutters around it like a bird.
—**Jules Renard,** *Journal*

To reason, to argue. It is to walk with crutches in search of the truth. We come to it with a leap.
—**Joseph Joubert,** *Notebooks*

The philosopher
Turns at dawn from his window into the room
And walks through it into another room
And then another one, as into deeper snow.
—**Allen Grossman,** "A Short Walk to the Human End"

Just as the wasteland and the wilderness are reconciled through earth's circuit of soil-building decay, the landscape and imagination may be united through the process of walking. The mind's flicker of attention from the earth to its own associations seems on one level to have an inescapably binary quality. But mental sunlight and clouds are also borne out under a larger sky in the meandering circuit of the poet's walk. Walking becomes an emblem of wholeness, comprehending both the person's conscious steps and pauses and the path beneath his rising and falling feet.

—**John Elder**, *Imagining the Earth*

Arrivals and Departures

Put your hand before your eyes and remember, you that have walked, the places from which you have walked away, and the wilderness into which you manfully turned the steps of your abandonment. . . . It is your business to leave all that you have known altogether behind you, and no man has eyes at the back of his head—go forward.

—**Hilaire Belloc,** Introduction to *The Footpath Way*

How fine it is to enter some old town, walled and turreted, just at the approach of nightfall, or to come to some straggling village, with the lights streaming through the surrounding gloom; and then after inquiring for the best entertainment that the place affords, to "take one's ease at one's inn!"

—**William Hazlitt,** "On Going a Journey"

Before modern times there was Walking, but not the perfection of Walking, because there was no tea.

—**George Macaulay Trevelyan,** "Walking"

Consider how a man walking approaches a little town; he sees it a long way off upon a hill; he sees its unity, he has time to think about it a great deal. Next it is hidden from him by a wood, or it is screened by a roll of land. He tops this and sees the little town again, now much nearer, and he thinks more particularly of its houses, of the way in which they stand, and of what has passed in them. The sky, especially if it has large white clouds in it and is for the rest sunlit and blue, makes something against which he can see the little town, and gives it life. Then he is at the outskirts, and he does not suddenly occupy it with a clamour or a rush, nor does he merely contemplate it, like a man from a window, unmoving. He enters in. He passes, healthily wearied, human doors and signs; he can note all the names of the people and the trade at which they work; he has time to see their faces. The square broadens before him, or the market-place, and so very naturally and rightly he comes to his inn, and he has fulfilled one of the great ends of man.

—**Hilaire Belloc,** Introduction to *The Footpath Way*

The more quickly he walked, the more he approached his house, the more it shrunk, became uninhabitable. The distance materialized behind his step and pushed him with the rhythm of a military troop that nothing hurries. He had to enter into this minimal house, which was impossible and became possible whenever the parade was stopped. The voyager, then, shrunk very fast while his house grew before his eye's view and a beautiful girl appeared at a window and laughed at his predicament.

—**Jean Cocteau,** "The Voyager"

Rooms are made to walk back into
After time is gone.
—**Paul Bowles,** "Acrostic Notice"

At the end of the long walk, your old dog dies of joy
whenever you sit down, a poor man at a fire.
—**Robert Lowell,** "The Walk"

As firmly cemented clam-shells
Fall apart in autumn,
So I must take to the road again,
Fare well, my friends.
—**Matsuo Bashō,** *The Narrow Road to the Deep North*

We should go forth on the shortest walk, perchance in
the spirit of undying adventure, never to return—prepared
to send back our embalmed hearts only as relics to our desolate kingdoms.
—**Henry David Thoreau,** "Walking"

Often as she listened to the pilgrims' tales she was so fired by their simple speech, natural to them but to her full of deep meaning, that several times she was on the point of abandoning everything and running away from home. In imagination she already pictured herself dressed in coarse rags and with her wallet and staff, walking along a dusty road.

—**Leo Tolstoy,** *War and Peace*

To throw away the key and walk away,
Not abrupt exile, the neighbours asking why,
But following a line with left and right
An altered gradient at another rate
Learns more than maps upon the whitewashed wall
The hand put up to ask; and makes us well
Without confession of the ill.

—**W. H. Auden,** "The Walking Tour"

Conversation

Moreover, I saw in my dream, that as they went on, Faithful, as he chanced to look on one side, saw a man whose name is Talkative, walking at a distance beside them; for in this place there was room enough for them all to walk. He was a tall man, and something more comely at a distance than at hand. To this man Faithful addressed himself in this manner:

FAITH. Friend, whither away? Are you going to the heavenly country?

TALK. I am going to the same place.

FAITH. That is well; then I hope we may have your good company.

TALK. With a very good will will I be your companion.

FAITH. Come on, then, and let us go together, and let us spend our time in discoursing of things that are profitable.

—**John Bunyan,** *The Pilgrim's Progress*

Last Sunday I took a Walk towards Highgate and in the lane that winds by the side of Lord Mansfield's park I met Mr Green our Demonstrator at Guy's in conversation with Coleridge—I joined them, after enquiring by a look whether it would be agreeable—I walked with him at his alderman-after-dinner pace for near two miles I suppose In those two Miles he broached a thousand things—let me see if I can give you a list—Nightingales, Poetry—on Poetical sensation—Metaphysics—Different genera and species of Dreams—Nightmare—a dream accompanied by a sense of touch—single and double touch—A dream related—First and second consciousness—the difference explained between will and Volition—so many metaphysicians from a want of smoking the second consciousness—Monsters—the Kraken—Mermaids—Southey believes in them—southeys belief too much diluted—A Ghost story—Good morning—I heard his voice as he came towards me—I heard it as he moved away—I heard it all the interval. . . .

—**John Keats,** letter to George and Georgiana Keats

My walk around the camp, the fires burning—groups around—the merry song—the sitting forms—the dying light on the faces—they would tell stories. . . . Went around among the camps—saw the hard accommodations and experiences of campaign life. . . . Went around mornings and evenings among the men—heard their conversation & —the bivouac fires at night, the singing and story-telling among the crowded crouching groups.

—**Walt Whitman,** notebooks

On Sundays Stephen with his father and his granduncle took their constitutional. The old man was a nimble walker in spite of his corns and often ten or twelve miles of the road were covered. The little village of Stillorgan was the parting of the ways. Either they went to the left towards the Dublin mountains or along the Goatstown road and thence into Dundrum, coming home by Sandyford. Trudging along the road or standing in some grimy wayside public-house his elders spoke constantly of the subjects nearer their hearts, of Irish politics, of Munster and of the legends of their own family, to all of which Stephen lent an avid ear. Words which he did not understand he said over and over to himself till he had learned them by heart: and through them he had glimpses of the real world about him. The hour when he too would take part in the life of that world seemed drawing near and in secret he began to make ready for the great part which he felt awaited him the nature of which he only dimly apprehended.

—**James Joyce,** *A Portrait of the Artist as a Young Man*

Walking for walking's sake may be as highly laudable and exemplary a thing as it is held to be by those who practise it. My objection to it is that it stops the brain. Many a man has professed to me that his brain never works so well as when he is swinging along the high road or over hill and dale. This boast is not confirmed by my memory of anybody who on a Sunday morning has forced me to partake of his adventure. Experience teaches me that whatever a fellow-guest may have of power to instruct or to amuse when he is sitting on a chair, or standing on a hearth-rug, quickly leaves him when he takes one out for a walk. The ideas that came so thick and fast to him in my room, where are they now? where that encyclopaedic knowledge which he bore so lightly? where the kindling fancy that played like summer lightning over *any* topic that was started? The man's face that was so mobile is set now; gone is the light from his fine eyes. He says that A. (our host) is a thoroughly good fellow. Fifty yards further on, he adds that A. is one of the best fellows he has ever met. We tramp another furlong or so, and he says that Mrs. A. is a charming woman. Presently he adds that she is one of the most charming women he has ever known. We pass an inn. He reads vapidly aloud to me: "The Kings Arms. Licensed to sell Ales and Spirits." I foresee that during the rest of the walk he will read aloud any inscription that occurs. We pass a milestone. He points at it with his stick, and says "Uxminster. 11 miles." We turn a sharp corner at the foot of a hill. He points at the wall, and says "Drive Slowly." I see far ahead, on the other side of the hedge bordering the high road, a small notice-board. He sees it too. He keeps his eye on it. And in due course "Trespassers," he says, "Will Be Prosecuted." Poor man!—mentally a wreck.

—Max Beerbohm, "Going Out for a Walk"

The stones, too, were silent. And it was quiet in the mountains where they walked, one and the other.

So it was quiet, quiet up in the mountains. But it was not quiet for long, because when a Jew comes along and meets another, silence cannot last, even in the mountains. Because the Jew and nature are strangers to each other, have always been and still are, even today, even here.

—**Paul Celan,** *Conversation in the Mountains*

At first as they stumped along the path which edged the Hundred Acre Wood, they didn't say much to each other; but when they came to the stream and had helped each other across the stepping stones, and were able to walk side by side again over the heather, they began to talk in a friendly way about this and that, and Piglet said, "If you see what I mean, Pooh," and Pooh said, "It's just what I think myself, Piglet," and Piglet said, "But, on the other hand, Pooh, we must remember," and Pooh said, "Quite true, Piglet, although I had forgotten it for the moment."

—**A. A. Milne,** *Winnie-the-Pooh*

Solitude

For in this walk, this voyage,
it is yourself, the profound history of your 'self,'
that now as always you encounter.
—**Conrad Aiken,** "The Walk in the Garden"

One of the pleasantest things in the world is going a journey; but I like to go by myself. I can enjoy society in a room; but out of doors, nature is company enough for me. I am then never less alone than when alone.

—**William Hazlitt,** "On Going a Journey"

When you are really walking the presence of a companion, involving such irksome considerations as whether the pace suits him, whether he wishes to go up by the rocks or down by the burn, still more the haunting fear that he may begin to talk, disturbs the harmony of body, mind, and soul when they stride along no longer conscious of their separate, jarring entities, made one together in mystic union with the earth, with the hills that still beckon, with the sunset that still shows the tufted moor under foot, with old darkness and its stars that take you to their breast with rapture when the hard ringing of heels proclaims that you have struck the final road.

—**George Macaulay Trevelyan,** "Walking"

The solitary, pensive walker draws a singular drunkenness from this universal communion. He who can easily blend into the crowd knows feverish pleasures, which will be eternally denied to the egoist, closed like a strong-box, and the sluggard, shut up like a mollusc. He adopts as his own all the professions, all the joys, and all the miseries that circumstances present to him.

—**Charles Baudelaire,** "Crowds"

Let the blow fall soon or late,
Let what will be o'er me;
Give the face of earth around,
And the road before me.

Wealth I ask not, hope nor love,
Nor a friend to know me;
All I ask, the heaven above
And the road below me.

—**Robert Louis Stevenson,** "The Vagabond"

The birds were flying all about the field; they fluttered up out of the grass at my feet as I walked along, so tame that I liked to think they kept some happy tradition from summer to summer of the safety of nests and good fellowship of mankind. Poor Joanna's house was gone except the stones of its foundations, and there was little trace of her flower garden except a single faded sprig of much-enduring French pinks, which a great bee and a yellow butterfly were befriending together. I drank at the spring, and thought that now and then some one would follow me from the busy, hard-worked, and simple-thoughted countryside of the mainland, which lay dim and dreamlike in the August haze, as Joanna must have watched it many a day. There was the world, and here was she with eternity well begun. In the life of each of us, I said to myself, there is a place remote and islanded, and given to endless regret or secret happiness; we are each the uncompanioned hermit and recluse of an hour or a day; we understand our fellows of the cell to whatever age of history they may belong.

—**Sarah Orne Jewett,** *The Country of the Pointed Firs*

It was her voice that made
The sky acutest at its vanishing.
She measured to the hour its solitude.
She was the single artificer of the world
In which she sang. And when she sang, the sea,
Whatever self it had, became the self
That was her song, for she was the maker. Then we,
As we beheld her striding there alone,
Knew that there never was a world for her
Except the one she sang and, singing, made.
—**Wallace Stevens,** "The Idea of Order at Key West"

Companionship

It is beneficial to walk through meadows, orchards, and woods with friends and companions, in flowering gardens where birds sing and nightingales are heard.

—**Valesco of Taranta**

Just a closer walk with Thee,
Grant it, Jesus, if you please.
—**Traditional spiritual**

Not one of us has the vaguest idea just how many mice there are in the world, it is unimaginable. The mice rustle very lightly in the flattened grass. Only he who walks sees these mice.

—**Werner Herzog,** *Of Walking in Ice*

On the other side of the river, a dense crowd of small, bright blue male butterflies that had been tippling on the rich, trampled mud and cow dung through which I trudged rose all together into the spangled air and settled again as soon as I had passed.

—**Vladimir Nabokov,** *Speak, Memory*

No domain of nature is quite closed to man at all times, and now we draw near to the empire of the fishes. Our feet glide swiftly over unfathomed depths, where in summer our line tempted the pout and perch, and where the stately pickerel lurked in the long corridors formed by the bulrushes. The deep, impenetrable marsh, where the heron waded and bittern squatted, is made pervious to our swift shoes, as if a thousand railroads had been made into it. With one impulse we are carried to the cabin of the muskrat, that earliest settler, and see him dart away under the transparent ice, like a furred fish, to his hole in the bank; and we glide rapidly over meadows where lately 'the mower whet his scythe,' through beds of frozen cranberries mixed with meadow-grass.

—**Henry David Thoreau,** "A Winter Walk"

The stag listened, scenting my words. When I was silent, he no longer hesitated: his legs moved like stalks crossed and uncrossed by the breeze.

—**Jules Renard,** *Histoires Naturelles*

The whole party were but just re-assembled in the drawing-room when Mr. Weston made his appearance among them. He had returned to a late dinner, and walked to Hartfield as soon as it was over. He had been too much expected by the best judges, for surprise—but there was great joy. . . . John Knightley only was in mute astonishment.—That a man who might have spent his evening quietly at home after a day of business in London, should set off again, and walk half-a-mile to another man's house, for the sake of being in mixed company till bedtime, of finishing his day in the efforts of civility and the noise of numbers, was a circumstance to strike him deeply. A man who had been in motion since eight o'clock in the morning, and might now have been still, who had been long talking, and might have been silent, who had been in more than one crowd, and might have been alone!—Such a man, to quit the tranquillity and independence of his own fireside, and on the evening of a cold sleety April day rush out again into the world!— . . . John Knightley looked at him with amazement, then shrugged his shoulders, and said, "I could not have believed it even of him."

—**Jane Austen,** *Emma*

A pedestrian seems in this country to be a sort of beast of passage—stared at, pitied, suspected and shunned by everybody who meets him. . . . Every passing coachman called out to me: "Do you want to ride on the outside?" If I met only a farm worker on a horse he would say to me companionably: "Warm walking, sir," and when I passed through a village the old women in their bewilderment would let out a "God Almighty!"

—**Carl Philip Moritz,** *Journeys of a German in England*

The mere sight of two strangers walking with such appendages as knapsacks strapped on their shoulders, seemed of itself to provide the most unbounded wonder. We were stared at with almost incredible pertinacity and good humour. People hard at work, left off to look at us; while groups congregated at cottage doors, walked into the middle of the road when they saw us approach, looked at us in front from that commanding point of view until we passed them, and then wheeled round with one accord and gazed at us behind as long as we were within sight. Little children ran in-doors to bring out large children, as we drew near. Farmers, overtaking us on horseback, pulled in, and passed at a walk, to examine us at their ease. With the exception of bedridden people and people in prison, I believe that the whole population of Cornwall looked at us all over—back view and front view—from head to foot!

 —**Wilkie Collins,** *Rambles beyond Railways*

We souls on foot, with foot-folk meet:
For we that cannot hope to ride
For ease or pride, have fellowship.
 —**William Barnes,** "Fellowship"

No fear of forgetting the good-humoured faces that meet us in our walks every day.

 —**Mary Russell Mitford,** *Our Village*

The pleasure of being in crowds is a mysterious expression of sensual joy in the multiplication of Number.

 —**Charles Baudelaire,** *Intimate Journals*

Next day we trudged along, but nothing very remarkable occurred excepting that we saw a fine black wolf quite tame and gentle, the owner of which refused a hundred dollars for it. Mr. Rose, who was an engineer, and a man of taste, amused us with his flageolet, which increased my good opinion of him. At an orchard we filled our pockets with October peaches, and when we came to Trade Water River we found it quite low. The acorns were already drifted on its shallows, and the Wood Ducks were running about picking them up. Passing a flat bottom, we saw a large Buffalo Lick. Where now are the bulls which erst scraped its earth away, bellowing forth their love or anger?

—**John James Audubon,** *Rambles on the Prairie*

Ordinarily, we seem to be completely separate from everything and everyone in our surroundings, and our sense of external things (if not of other people) is that they are waiting around until we can find something for them to do. At moments when the boundaries flow together, perhaps even disappear, a different sense emerges. Walking through a landscape, we have the sense that the plants and animals around us have purposes of their own. At the same time, our sense of ourselves now has more to do with noticing how we are connected to the people and things around us—as part of a family, a crowd, a community, a species, a biosphere.

—**Tony Hiss,** "Experiencing Places"

She walks down Garden Avenue to a small grocery store which sells penny candy. Three pennies are in her shoe—slipping back and forth between the sock and the inner sole. With each step she feels the painful press of the coins against her foot. A sweet, endurable, even cherished irritation, full of promise and delicate security. There is plenty of time to consider what to buy. Now, however, she moves down an avenue gently buffeted by the familiar and therefore loved images. . . .

There was the sidewalk crack shaped like a Y, and the other one that lifted the concrete up from the dirt floor. Frequently her sloughing step had made her trip over that one. Skates would go well over this sidewalk—old it was, and smooth; it made the wheels glide evenly, with a mild whirr. The newly paved walks were bumpy and uncomfortable, and the sound of skate wheels on new walks was grating.

These and other inanimate things she saw and experienced. They were real to her. She knew them. They were the codes and touchstones of the world, capable of translation and possession. She owned the crack that made her stumble; she owned the clumps of dandelions whose white heads, last fall, she had blown away; whose yellow heads, this fall, she peered into. And owning them made her part of the world, and the world a part of her.

—**Toni Morrison,** *The Bluest Eye*

Love

I will rise now, and go about the city in the streets, and in the broad ways I will seek him whom my soul loveth.

—Song of Solomon 3:2

I must go walk the wood so wild,
   And wander here and there
   In dread and deadly fear;
For where I trusted I am beguiled,
   And all for one.

Thus am I banished from my bliss
   By craft and false pretense,
   Faultless without offense,
As of return no certain is,
   And all for fear of one.

My bed shall be under the greenwood tree,
   A tuft of brakes under my bed,
   As one from Joy were fled;
Thus from my life day by day I flee,
   And all for one.

The running streams shall be my drink,
   Acorns shall be my food;
   Nothing may do me good,
But when of your beauty I do think,
   And all for love of one.
—**Anonymous,** "The Banished Lover"

From thought to thought, from mountain peak to mountain
Love leads me on; for I can never still
My trouble on the world's well-beaten ways.
—**Petrarch,** Ode 17

. . . the doctors of antiquity have affirmed that love is a passion that resembles the melancholy disease. The physician Rasis prescribeds, therefore, in order to recover, coitus, fasting, drunkenness, walking.
—**Marsilio Ficino,** *De Amore*

Keep on walkin' and walkin', talkin' to myself. Keep on walkin' and walkin', talkin' to myself. Gal I love's with somebody else. I'm goin' find my baby, don't think she can be found. I'm goin' find my baby, don't think she can be found. Goin' walk this hard road till my moustache drag the ground.
—**Blind Arthur Blake,** "Hard Road Blues"

But oh! how bless'd would be the day,
Did I with Clio pace my way,
And not alone and solitary stray!
—**John Dyer,** "The Country Walk"

Those who have read any Romance or Poetry ancient or modern, must have been informed, that Love hath Wings; by which they are not to understand, as some young Ladies by mistake have done, that a Lover can fly: the Writers, by this ingenious Allegory, intending to insinuate no more, than that Lovers do not march like Horse-Guards; in short, that they put the best Leg foremost, which our lusty Youth, who could walk with any Man, did so heartily on this Occasion, that within four Hours, he reached the famous House of Hospitality well known to the Western Traveller. It presents you a Lion on the Sign-Post: and the Master, who was christened *Timotheus,* is commonly called plain *Tim*.

—**Henry Fielding,** *Joseph Andrews*

Say maiden can thy life be led
To join the living with the dead
Then trace thy footsteps on with me
We're wed to one eternity
—**John Clare,** "An Invite to Eternity"

. . . Miss Bingley began abusing her as soon as she was out of the room. Her manners were pronounced to be very bad indeed, a mixture of pride and impertinence: she had no conversation, no style, no taste, no beauty. Mrs. Hurst thought the same, and added:

"She has nothing, in short, to recommend her, but being an excellent walker. I shall never forget her appearance this morning. She really looked almost wild."

"She did, indeed, Louisa. I could hardly keep my countenance. Very nonsensical to come at all! Why must *she* be scampering about the country, because her sister had a cold? Her hair, so untidy, so blowsy!"

"Yes, and her petticoat; I hope you saw her petticoat, six inches deep in mud, I am absolutely certain; and the gown which had been let down to hide it not doing its office."

"Your picture may be very exact, Louisa," said Bingley;

"but this was all lost upon me. I thought Miss Elizabeth Bennet looked remarkably well when she came into the room this morning. Her dirty petticoat quite escaped my notice."

"You observed it, Mr. Darcy, I am sure," said Miss Bingley; "and I am inclined to think that you would not wish to see *your sister* make such an exhibition."

"Certainly not."

"To walk three miles, or four miles, or five miles, or whatever it is, above her ankles in dirt, and alone, quite alone! what could she mean by it? It seems to me to show an abominable sort of conceited independence, a most country-town indifference to decorum."

"It shows an affection for her sister that is very pleasing," said Bingley.

"I am afraid, Mr. Darcy," observed Miss Bingley, in a half whisper, "that this adventure has rather affected your admiration of her fine eyes."

"Not at all," he replied; "they were brightened by the exercise."

—**Jane Austen,** *Pride and Prejudice*

At night walking along the streets, the darker because
of trees,
we came to a tree, white with flowers,
and the pavement under the branches was white with
flowers too.
Had I the heavens' embroidered cloths . . .
I would spread the cloths under your feet:
But I, being poor, have only my dreams;
I have spread my dreams under your feet;
Tread softly because you tread on my dreams.
—**W. B. Yeats,** "He Wishes for the Cloths of Heaven"

My gentle friend, my merciless enemy, your every step
carries such blessing
That you might be walking along my heart, scattering
stars and flowers.
—**Nikolai S. Gumilev,** "She Who Scatters Stars"

As I went down the hill along the wall
There was a gate I had leaned at for the view
And had just turned from when I first saw you
As you came up the hill. We met. But all
We did that day was mingle great and small
Footprints in summer dust as if we drew
The figure of our being less than two
But more than one as yet.
—**Robert Frost,** "Meeting and Passing"

If Beale Street could talk,
If Beale Street could talk,
Married men would have to take their babes
And walk.
—**W. C. Handy,** "Beale Street Blues"

Work

. . . there you have the secret of good work: to plod on and still keep the passion fresh.

—**George Meredith,** *The Egoist*

Whether I walked with the young ladies or rode with their parents, depended entirely upon their own capricious will: if they chose to "take" me, I went; if, for reasons best known to themselves, they chose to go alone, I took my seat in the carriage: I liked walking better, but a sense of reluctance to obtrude my presence on any one who did not desire it, always kept me passive on these and similar occasions; and I never inquired into the causes of their varying whims and indeed, this was the best policy—for to submit and oblige was the governess's part, to consult their own pleasure was that of the pupils. But when I did walk, this first half of the journey was generally a great nuisance to me. . . . Thus—I am almost ashamed to confess it—but indeed I gave myself no little trouble in my endeavours (if I did keep up with them) to appear perfectly unconscious or regardless of their presence, as if I were wholly absorbed in my own reflections, or the contemplation of surrounding objects; or, if I lingered behind, it was some bird or insect, some tree or flower, that attracted my attention, and having duly examined that, I would pursue my walk alone, at a leisurely pace, until my pupils had bid adieu to their companions, and turned off into the quiet, private road.

—**Anne Brontë,** *Agnes Grey*

The Paper Mill had stopped work for the night, and the paths and roads in its neighbourhood were sprinkled with clusters of people going home from their day's labour in it. There were men, women, and children in the groups, and there was no want of lively colour to flutter in the gentle evening wind. The mingling of various voices and the sound of laughter made a cheerful impression upon the ear, analogous to that of the fluttering colours upon the eye. Into the sheet of water reflecting the flushed sky in the foreground of the living picture, a knot of urchins were casting stones, and watching the expansion of the rippling circles. So, in the rosy evening, one might watch the ever-widening beauty of the landscape—beyond the newly-released workers wending home—beyond the silver river—beyond the deep green fields of corn, so prospering, that the loiterers in their narrow threads of pathway seemed to float immersed breast-high—beyond the hedgerows and the clumps of trees—beyond the windmills on the ridge—away to where the sky appeared to meet the earth, as if there were no immensity of space between mankind and Heaven.

—**Charles Dickens,** *Our Mutual Friend*

At this moment I resolved, for the first time, to go to my master, enter a complaint, and ask his protection. In order to do this, I must that afternoon walk seven miles; and this, under the circumstances, was truly a severe undertaking. I was exceedingly feeble; made so as much by the kicks and blows which I received, as by the severe fit of sickness to which I had been subjected. I, however, watched my chance, while Covey was looking in an opposite direction, and started for St. Michael's. I succeeded in getting a considerable distance on my way to the woods, when Covey discovered me, and called after me to come back, threatening what he would do if I did not come. I disregarded both his calls and his threats, and made my way to the woods as fast as my feeble state would allow; and thinking I might be overhauled by him if I kept the road, I walked through the woods, keeping far enough from the road to avoid detection, and near enough to prevent losing my way. I had not gone far before my little strength again failed me. I could go no farther. I fell down, and lay for a considerable time. The blood was yet oozing from the wound on my head. For a time I thought I should bleed to death; and think now that I should have done so, but that the blood so matted my hair as to stop the wound. After lying there about three quarters of an hour, I nerved myself up again, and started on my way, through bogs and briers, barefooted and bareheaded, tearing my feet sometimes at nearly every step; and after a journey of about seven miles, occupying some five hours to perform it, I arrived at master's store.

—**Frederick Douglass,** *Narrative of an American Slave*

One says to me, "I wonder that you do not lay up money; you love to travel; you might take the cars and go to Fitchburg to-day and see the country." But I am wiser than that. I have learned that the swiftest traveller is he that goes afoot. I say to my friend, Suppose we try who will get there first. The distance is thirty miles; the fare ninety cents. That is almost a day's wages. I remember when wages were sixty cents a day for laborers on this very road. Well, I start now on foot, and get there before night; I have travelled at that rate by the week together. You will in the mean while have earned your fare, and arrive there some time to-morrow, or possibly this evening, if you are lucky enough to get a job in season. Instead of going to Fitchburg, you will be working here the greater part of the day. And so, if the railroad reached round the world, I think that I should keep ahead of you; and as for seeing the country and getting experience of that kind, I should have to cut your acquaintance altogether.

—**Henry David Thoreau,** *Walden*

Today I know there is nothing beyond the farthest of far ridges except a sign-post to unknown places. The end is in the means—in the sight of that beautiful long straight line of the Downs in which a curve is latent—in the houses we shall never enter, with their dark secret windows and quiet hearth smoke, or their ruins friendly only to elders and nettles—in the people passing whom we shall never know though we may love them. Today I know that I walk because it is necessary to do so in order both to live and to make a living.

—**Edward Thomas,** "A Fellow Walker"

with little money in a great city.
There's snow in every street
Where I go up and down,
And there's no woman, man, or dog
That knows me in the town.

I know each shop, and all
These Jews, and Russian Poles,
For I go walking night and noon
To spare my sack of coals.
—**John M. Synge,** "Winter"

I asked the veteran traveller to tell me the best place to harvest. . . . "Go straight west," he said, "to Great Bend, Barton County, Kansas, the banner wheat country of the United States. Arrive about July fifth. Walk to the public square. Walk two miles north. Look around. You will see nothing but wheat fields, and farmers standing on the edge of the road crying into big red handkerchiefs. Ask the first man for work. He will stop crying and give it to you. Wages will be two dollars and a half a day, and keep. You will have all you want to eat and a clean blanket in the hay."

I resolved to harvest at Great Bend.

—**Vachel Lindsey,** *Adventures while Preaching the
Gospel of Beauty*

Literature and Art

The labor of scribbling books happily leaves no distinct impression, and I would forget that it had ever been undergone; but the picture of some delightful ramble includes incidentally a reference to the nightmare of literary toil from which it relieved me. The author is but the accidental appendage of the tramp.

—**Leslie Stephen,** "In Praise of Walking"

For Dr. Johnson and George Borrow, both great wanderers in their time, making contact with the world took on a quite literal meaning during their walks. Both were dogged by recurrent bouts of depression, and to keep some kind of link with reality used to touch objects—trees especially—on their way.

—**Richard Mobey,** "A Walk around the Block"

At present he [William] is out walking and has been out of doors these two hours though it has rained heavily all the morning. In wet weather he takes out an umbrella; chuses the most sheltered spot, and there walks backwards and forwards and though the length of his walk be sometimes a quarter or half a mile, he is as fast bound within the chosen limits as if by prison walls. He generally composes his verses out of doors and while he is so engaged he seldom knows how the time slips by or hardly whether it is rain or fair.

—**Dorothy Wordsworth,** letter

I calculate, upon good data, that with these identical legs Wordsworth must have traversed a distance of 175,000 or 180,000 English miles, a mode of exertion which to him stood in the stead of alcohol and all stimulants whatsoever to the animal spirits; to which indeed he was indebted for a life of unclouded happiness, and we for what is most excellent in his writings.

—**Thomas De Quincey,** "Recollections of the Lake Poets"

I have always fancied that walking as a fine art was not much practiced before the Eighteenth Century. We know from Ambassador Jussurand's famous book how many wayfarers were abroad on the roads in the Fourteenth Century, but none of these were abroad for the pleasures of moving meditation and scenery. . . . Generally speaking, it is true that cross-country walks for the pure delight of rhythmically placing one foot before the other were rare before Wordsworth. I always think of him as one of the first to employ his legs as an instrument of philosophy.

—**Christopher Morley,** "The Art of Walking"

For good Wordsworthians—and most serious-minded people are now Wordsworthians—either by direct inspiration or at second hand—a walk in the country is the equivalent of going to church, a tour though Westmoreland is as good as a pilgrimage to Jerusalem.

—**Aldous Huxley,** "Wordsworth in the Tropics"

I purpose within a month to put a knapsack at my back and make a pedestrian tour through the north of England, and part of Scotland—to make a sort of prologue to the life I intend to pursue—that is to write, to study, and to see all of Europe at the lowest expense. I will clamber through the clouds and exist.

—**John Keats,** letter

striding down my orchard & homesteed I hum & sing inwardly those little madrigals & then go in & pen them down. . . & so in spite of myself I rhyme on & write nothing but little things at last.

—**John Clare,** letter to H. F. Cary, October 1832

"It was on the 10th of April, 1798," says Hazlitt, with amorous precision, "that I sat down to a volume of the new *Heloise,* at the Inn at Llangollen, over a bottle of sherry and cold chicken." I should wish to quote more, for though we are mighty fine fellows nowadays, we cannot write like Hazlitt. And, talking of that, a volume of Hazlitt's essays would be a capital pocket-book on such a journey; so would a volume of Heine's songs; and for *Tristram Shandy* I can pledge a fair experience.

—**Robert Louis Stevenson,** "Walking Tours"

Charlotte told me, that, at this period of her life, drawing, and walking out with her sisters, formed the two great pleasures and relaxations of her day. The three girls used to walk upwards towards the "purple-black" moors, the sweeping surface of which was broken by here and there a stone-quarry; and if they had strength and time to go far enough, they reached a waterfall, where the beck fell over some rocks into the "bottom." They seldom went downwards through the village. They were shy of meeting even familiar faces, and were scrupulous about entering the house of the very poorest uninvited. They were steady teachers at the Sunday-school, a habit which Charlotte kept up very faithfully, even after she was left alone; but they never faced their kind voluntarily, and always preferred the solitude and freedom of the moors.

—**Elisabeth Gaskell,** *Life of Charlotte Brontë*

Baudelaire saw fit to equate the man of the crowd, whom Poe's narrator [in his story "The Man of the Crowd"] follows throughout the length and breadth of nocturnal London, with the *flaneur*. It is hard to accept this view. The man of the crowd is no *flaneur*. In him, composure has given way to manic behavior. Hence he exemplifies, rather, what had to become of the *flaneur* once he was deprived of the milieu to which he belonged. If London ever provided it for him, it was certainly not the setting described by Poe. In comparison, Baudelaire's Paris preserved some features that dated back to the happy old days. Ferries were still crossing the Seine at points that would later be spanned by the arch of a bridge. In the year of Baudelaire's death it was still possible for some entrepreneur to cater to the comfort of the well-to-do with a fleet of five hundred sedan chairs circulating about the city. Arcades where the *flaneur* would not be exposed to the sight of carriages that did not recognize pedestrians as rivals were enjoying undiminished popularity. There was the pedestrian who would let himself be jostled by the crowd, but there was also the *flaneur* who demanded elbow room and was unwilling to forgo the life of a gentleman of leisure. Let the many attend to their daily affairs; the man of leisure can indulge in the perambulations of the *flaneur* only if as such he is already out of place. He is as much out of place in an atmosphere of complete leisure as in the feverish turmoil of the city.

—**Walter Benjamin,** "On Some Motifs in Baudelaire"

In the far South the sun of autumn is passing
Like Walt Whitman walking along a ruddy shore.
He is singing and chanting the things that are part
    of him,
The worlds that were and will be, death and day.
Nothing is final, he chants. No man shall see the end.
His beard is of fire and his staff is a leaping flame.
—**Wallace Stevens,** "Like Decorations in
               a Nigger Cemetery"

Where are we going, Walt Whitman? The doors close in an hour. Which way does your beard point tonight?

(I touch your book and dream of our odyssey in the supermarket and feel absurd.)

Will we walk all night through solitary streets? The trees add shade to shade, lights out in the houses, we'll both be lonely.

Will we stroll dreaming of the lost America of love past blue automobiles in driveways, home to our silent cottage?

—**Allen Ginsberg,** "A Supermarket in California"

Then one day walking around Tavistock Square I made up, as I sometimes make up my books, *To the Lighthouse*, in a great, apparently involuntary rush.

—**Virginia Woolf,** *Moments of Being*

[Nanao Sakaki's] poems were not written by hand or head, but with the feet. These poems have been sat into existence, walking into existence, to be left here as traces of a life lived for living—not for intellect or culture. And so the intellect is deep, the culture profound.

—**Gary Snyder,** "Walked into Existence"

Let me walk through the fields of paper
touching with my wand
dry stems and stunted
butterflies—

—**Denise Levertov,** "A Walk through the Notebooks"

The walking of passers-by offers a series of turns and detours that can be compared to "turns of phrase" or "stylistic figures." There is a rhetoric of walking. The art of "turning" phrases finds an equivalent in an art of composing a path.

—**Michel de Certeau,** "Walking in the City"

What if walking ceases to be a popular, cheap entertainment, and becomes "virtuous," something good for you, a cultural duty? Would it hold the same appeal for young writers? Will future literary meditations all take place from behind the wheel? Or is there an intrinsic, powerfully organic connection between walking and writing, pen and foot, which will survive the suburbanization and homogenization of city life? I would like to think that the more urban civilization changes, the more we will need a literature to reflect these shifts, with fine-grained descriptions at street level, such as can only be provided by a walker's unhurried perspective.

—**Phillip Lopate**, "The Pen on Foot: The Literature of Walking Around"

You could not play-act into the past, you could not turn it into a game of make-believe. There had to be another way. Somehow you had to produce the living effect, while remaining true to the dead fact. The adult distance—the critical distance, the historical distance—had to be maintained. You stood at the end of the broken bridge and looked across carefully, objectively, into the unattainable past on the other side. You brought it alive, brought it back, by other sorts of skills and crafts and sensible magic.

Have I explained myself at all? It is the simplicity of the idea, the realisation, that I am after. . . . "Biography" meant a book about someone's life. Only, for me, it was to become a kind of pursuit, a tracking of the physical trail of someone's path through the past, a following of footsteps. You would never catch them; no, you would never quite catch them. But maybe, if you were lucky, you might write about the pursuit of that fleeting figure in such a way as to bring it alive in the present.

—**Richard Holmes,** *Footsteps*

I have come to believe that all essays walk in rivers. Essays ask the philosophical question that flows through time—How shall I live my life? The answers drift together through countless converging streams, where they move softly below the reflective surface of the natural world and mix in the deep and quiet places of the mind. This is where an essayist must walk, stirring up the mud.

—**Kathleen Dean Moore,** *Riverwalking*

. . . a novel is a mirror journeying down the high road. Sometimes it reflects to your view the azure blue of heaven, sometimes the mire in the puddles on the road below. And the man who carries the mirror in his pack will be accused by you of being immoral! His mirror reflects the mire, and you blame the mirror! Blame rather the high road on which the puddle lies, and still more the inspector of roads and highways who lets the water stand there and the puddle form.

—**Stendhal,** *Scarlet and Black*

How does a poem resemble a walk? First, each makes use of the whole body, involvement is total, both mind and body. You can't take a walk without feet and legs, without a circulatory system, a guidance and co-ordinating system, without eyes, ears, desire, will, need: the total person.

—**A. R. Ammons,** "A Poem Is a Walk"

—a present, a "present"
world, across three states (Ben Shahn saw it

among its rails and wires,
and noted it down) walked across three states
for it . .
a secret world,
a sphere, a snake with its tail in
its mouth
  rolls backward into the past
—**William Carlos Williams,** *Paterson*

He is pruned of every gesture, saving only
The habit of coming and going. Every pace
Shuffles a million feet.
—**Richard Wilbur,** on Giacometti's *Man Walking*

A walk marks time with an accumulation of footsteps. It
defines the form of the land. Walking the roads and paths is
to trace a portrait of the country. I have become interested in
using a walk to express original ideas about the land, art,
and walking itself.
—**Richard Long,** "Words after the Fact"

Life Is a Journey

The walk magnified is the journey, and probably no figure has been used more often than the journey for both the structure and the concern of an interior seeking.

—**A. R. Ammons,** "A Poem Is a Walk"

Midway in the journey of our life I found myself in a dark wood, for the straight way was lost. Ah, how hard it is to tell what that wood was, wild, rugged, harsh; the very thought of it renews the fear! It is so bitter that death is hardly more so. But, to treat of the good that I found in it, I will tell of the other things I saw there.

—**Dante Alighieri,** *Inferno*, trans. Charles S. Singleton

One summertime, when the sun was mild, I dressed myself in sheepskin clothing, the habit of a hermit of unholy life, and wandered abroad in this world, listening out for its strange and wonderful events. But one May morning, on Malvern Hills, out of the unknown, a marvellous thing happened to me. I was tired out after wandering astray, and I turned aside to rest under a spacious bank beside a stream. And as I lay down and leaned back, and looked into the water, I grew drowsy and fell asleep, so sweet was the music that it made.

—**William Langland,** *Piers Plowman,*
trans. A. V. C. Schmidt

As I walked through the wilderness of this world, I lighted on a certain place, where was a den; and I laid me down in that place to sleep: and as I slept I dreamed a dream. I dreamed, and behold I saw a man clothed with rags, standing in a certain place, with his face from his own house, a book in his hand, and a great burden upon his back. I looked, and saw him open the book, and read therein; and as he read, he wept and trembled: and not being able longer to contain, he brake out with a lamentable cry; saying, "What shall I do?"

—**John Bunyan**, *The Pilgrim's Progress*

With light step, as if earth and its trammels had little power to restrain him, a young man ["The Fool" (Tarot)] in gorgeous vestments pauses at the brink of a precipice among the great heights of the world; he surveys the blue distance before him—its expanse of sky rather than the prospect below. His act of eager walking is still indicated, though he is stationary at the given moment; his dog is still bounding. The edge which opens on the depth has no terror; it is as if angels were waiting to behold him, if it came about that he leaped from the height. His countenance is full of intelligence and expectant dream. . . . He is a prince of the other world on his travels through this one—all amidst the morning glory, in the keen air. The sun, which shines behind him, knows whence he came, whither he is going, and how he will return by another path after many days. He is the spirit in search of experience.

—**Arthur Edward Waite,** *The Pictorial Key to the Tarot*

Stranger to civil and religious rage,
The good man walked innoxious through his age.

—**Alexander Pope,** "Epistle to Arbuthnot"

. . . just now as I was crossing the boulevard in a great hurry, splashing through the mud in the midst of a seething chaos, and with death galloping at me from every side, I gave a sudden start and my halo slipped off my head and fell into the mire of the macadam. I was far too frightened to pick it up. I decided it was less unpleasant to lose my insignia than to get my bones broken. Then, too, I reflected, every cloud has its silver lining. I can now go about incognito, be as low as I please and indulge in debauch like ordinary mortals.

—**Charles Baudelaire,** *Paris Spleen*

There is . . . this consolation to the most wayworn traveler, upon the dustiest road, that the path his feet describe is so perfectly symbolical of human life,—now climbing the hills, now descending into the vales. From the summits he beholds the heavens and the horizon, from the vales he looks up to the heights again. He is treading his old lessons still, and though he may be very weary and travel-worn, it is a yet sincere experience.

—**Henry David Thoreau,** "A Walk to Wachusett"

She had plenty of leisure now, day in, day out, to survey her life as a tract of country traversed, and at last become a landscape instead of separate fields or separate years and days, so that it became a unity and she could see the whole view, and could even pick out a particular field and wander round it again in spirit, though seeing it all the while as it were from a height, fallen into its proper place, with the exact pattern drawn round it by the hedge, and the next field into which the gap in the hedge would lead. So, she thought, could she at last put circles round her life. Slowly she crossed that day, as one crosses a field by a little path through the grasses, with the sorrel and the buttercups waving on either side; she crossed it again slowly, from breakfast to bedtime, and each hour, as one hand of the clock passed over the other regained for her its separate character. . . .

—**Vita Sackville-West,** *All Passion Spent*

If you were walking across a plain, had an honest intention of walking on, and yet kept regressing, then it would be a desperate matter; but since you are scrambling up a cliff, about as steep as you yourself are if seen from below, the regression can only be caused by the nature of the ground, and you must not despair.

—**Franz Kafka,** *Notebooks*

"To stop on the road would mean to favor this road at the expense of another. I move on, unsure. The future, I now know, leaves no trace."

"And yet you will die on the road."

"What is death where there are no more roads?"

"Perhaps expectation, perhaps also oblivion of roads; night of unsayable and absurd wandering."

—**Edmond Jabes,** *The Book of Margins*

The best thing is to walk. We should follow the Chinese poet Li Po in "the hardships of travel and the many branchings of the way." For life is a journey through a wilderness. This concept, universal to the point of banality, could not have survived unless it were biologically true. None of our revolutionary heroes is worth a thing until he has been on a good walk. Che Guevara spoke of the "nomadic phase" of the Cuban Revolution. Look what the Long March did for Mao Tse-Tung, or Exodus for Moses.

—**Bruce Chatwin,** "It's a Nomad Nomad World"

That's one small step for a man, one giant leap for mankind.

—Neil Armstrong

J oy

It is hard if I cannot start some game on these lone heaths. I laugh, I run, I leap, I sing for joy. From the point of view of yonder rolling cloud, I plunge into my past being, and revel there, as the sun-burnt Indian plunges headlong into the wave that wafts him to his native shore. Then long-forgotten things, like 'sunken wrack and sumless treasuries,' burst upon my eager sight, and I begin to feel, think, and be myself again.

—**William Hazlitt,** "On Going a Journey"

Happily the spell is taken off for me
Happily I walk, impervious to pain I walk,
Light within I walk, joyous I walk
... In beauty I walk
With beauty before me I walk
With beauty after me I walk
With beauty above me I walk
With beauty above and about me I walk
It is finished in beauty
It is finished in beauty
—**Navajo tribe,** *The Night Chant*

Those walks did now like a returning spring
Come back on me again. When first I made
Once more the circuit of our little lake
If ever happiness hath lodged with man
That day consummate happiness was mine—
Wide-spreading, steady, calm, contemplative.
The sun was set, or setting, when I left
Our cottage door, and evening soon brought on
A sober hour, not winning or serene,
For cold and raw the air was, and untuned;
But as a face we love is sweetest then

When sorrow damps it, or, whatever look
It chance to wear, is sweetest if the heart
Have fulness in itself, even so with me
It fared that evening. Gently did my soul
Put off her veil, and self-transmuted, stood
Naked as in the presence of her God.
As on I walked, a comfort seemed to touch
A heart that had not been disconsolate,
Strength came where weakness was not known to be,
At least not felt; and restoration came
Like an intruder knocking at the door
Of unacknowledged weariness.
—**William Wordsworth,** *The Prelude*

January 31, 1854.—A walk: the air incredibly pure, delights for the eye, a warm and gently caressing sunlight, one's whole being joyous. A spring-like charm. Felt to my marrow this purifying, moving influence, laden with poetry and tenderness; had a strong religious feeling of gratitude and wonder. Seated motionless on a bench in the Tranchees, beside the ditches with their garb of moss, carpeted with grass, I felt intensely, delightfully alive.

—**Henri Frederic Amiel,** "What a Lovely Walk!"

I stayed at home and walked in the little garden to be alone in my joy.

—**Joseph Joubert,** *Notebooks*

I walk, I lift up, I lift up heart, eyes,
  Down all that glory in the heavens to glean our Saviour;
  And, éyes, heárt, what looks, what lips yet gave you a
Rapturous love's greeting of realer, of rounder replies?

—**Gerard Manley Hopkins,** "Hurrahing in Harvest"

In the course of a day's walk, you see, there is much variance in the mood. From the exhilaration of the start, to the happy phlegm of the arrival, the change is certainly great. As the day goes on, the traveller moves from the one extreme toward the other. He becomes more and more incorporated with the material landscape, and the open-air drunkenness grows upon him with great strides, until he posts along the road, and sees everything about him, as in a cheerful dream.

—**Robert Louis Stevenson,** "Walking Tours"

On and on and on he strode, far out over the sands, singing wildly to the sea, crying to greet the advent of the life that had cried to him.

Her image had passed into his soul for ever and no word had broken the holy silence of his ecstasy. Her eyes had called him and his soul had leaped at the call. To live, to err, to fall, to triumph, to recreate life out of life! A wild angel had appeared to him, the angel of mortal youth and beauty, an envoy from the fair courts of life, to throw open before him in an instance of ecstasy the gates of all the ways of error and glory. On and on and on and on!

—**James Joyce,** *A Portrait of the Artist as a Young Man*

"Friday I tasted life," said Emily Dickinson, the American Blake. "It was a vast morsel." Something of that baffled exultation seizes one in certain moments of strolling, when the afternoon sun streams down Chestnut Street on the homeward pressing crowd, or in clear crisp mornings as one walks through Washington Square.

—**Christopher Morley,** "Sauntering"

Walking I am unbound, and find that precious unity of life and imagination, that silent outgoing of self, which is so easy to lose, but which at high moments seems to start up again from the deepest rhythms of my own body. How often have I had this longing for an infinite walk—of going unimpeded, until the movement of my body as I walked fell into the flight of streets under my feet—until I in my body and the world in its skin of earth were blended into a single act of knowing!

—**Alfred Kazin,** "The Open Street"

Putting facts by the thousands,
into the world, the toes take off
with an appealing squeak which the thumping heel
follows confidentially, the way men greet men.
Sometimes walking is just such elated
pumping.

—**Lyn Hejinian,** "Determination"

Sorrow

I woke up this mornin', feelin' round for my shoes
Know 'bout 'at I got these, old walkin' blues.
—**Robert Johnson,** "Walkin' Blues"

Desperation is so named because it lacks the foot *(pes)* to walk in the way that is Christ.

—**Paschasius Radbertus,** quoted in

Giorgio Agamben, *Stanzas*

Madam, an hour before the worshipped sun
Peered forth the golden window of the east,
A troubled mind drove me to walk abroad,
Where, underneath the grove of sycamore
That westward rooteth from this city side,
So early walking did I see your son.
Towards him I made, but he was ware of me
And stole into the covert of the wood.
I, measuring his affections by my own,
Which then most sought where most might not be found,
Being one too many by my weary self,
Pursued my humour not pursuing his,
And gladly shunned who gladly fled from me.

—**William Shakespeare,** *Romeo and Juliet*

I resolved to go alone to the summit of Montavert. . . . The ascent is precipitous, but the path is cut into continual and short windings, which enable you to surmount the perpendicularity of the mountain. It is a scene terrifically desolate. In a thousand spots the traces of the winter avalanche may be perceived, where trees lie broken and strewed on the ground; some entirely destroyed, others bent, leaning upon the jutting rocks of the mountain, or transversely upon other trees. The path, as you ascend higher, is intersected by ravines of snow, down which stones continually roll from above; one of them is particularly dangerous, as the slightest sound, such as even speaking in a loud voice, produces a concussion of air sufficient to draw destruction upon the head of the speaker. The pines are not tall or luxuriant, but they are sombre, and add an air of severity to the scene. I looked on the valley beneath; vast mists were rising from the rivers which ran through it, and added to the melancholy impression I received from the objects around me. Alas! why does man boast of sensibilities superior to those apparent in the brute; it only renders them more necessary beings. If our impulses were confined to hunger, thirst, and desire, we might be nearly free; but now we are moved by every wind that blows, and a chance word or scene that that word may convey to us.

We rest; a dream has power to poison sleep.
We rise, one wand'ring thought pollutes the day.
We feel, conceive, or reason; laugh, or weep,
Embrace fond woe, or cast our cares away;
It is the same: for, be it joy or sorrow,
The path of its departure still is free.
Man's yesterday may ne'er be like his morrow;
Nought may endure but mutability!
—**Mary Shelley** / **Percy Shelley**, *Frankenstein*

The path by which we twain did go,
Which led by tracts that pleased us well,
Thro' four sweet years arose and fell,
From flower to flower, from snow to snow;

And we with singing cheer'd the way,
And, crown'd with all the season lent,
From April on to April went,
And glad at heart from May to May;

But where the path we walk'd began
To slant the fifth autumnal slope,

As we descended following Hope,
There sat the Shadow fear'd of man;

Who broke our fair companionship,
And spread his mantle dark and cold,
And wrapt thee formless in the fold,
And dull'd the murmur on thy lip;

And bore thee where I could not see
Nor follow, tho' I walk in haste,
And think, that somewhere in the waste
The Shadow sits and waits for me.
—**Alfred Lord Tennyson,** *In Memoriam: A. H. H.*

For the first few miles out of Stoniton, she walked on bravely, always fixing on some tree or gate or projecting bush at the most distant visible point in the road as a goal, and feeling a faint joy when she had reached it. But when she came to the fourth milestone, the first she had happened to notice among the long grass by the roadside, and read that she was still only four miles beyond Stoniton, her courage sank. She had come only this little way, and yet felt tired, and almost hungry again in the keen morning air; for though Hetty was accustomed to much movement and exertion indoors, she was not used to long walks which produced quite a different sort of fatigue from that of household activity. As she was looking at the milestone she felt some drops falling on her face—it was beginning to rain. Here was a new trouble which had not entered into her sad thoughts before, and quite weighed down by this sudden addition to her burden, she sat down on the step of a stile and began to sob hysterically. The beginning of hardship is like the first taste of bitter food—it seems for a moment unbearable; yet, if there is nothing else to satisfy our hunger, we take another bite and find it possible to go on.

—**George Eliot,** *Adam Bede*

At four o'clock that Sunday morning she came downstairs and stepped out into the starlight. The weather was still favourable, the ground ringing under her feet like an anvil. . . . It was a year ago all but a day that Clare had married Tess, and only a few days less than a year that he had been absent from her. Still, to start on a brisk walk, and on such an errand as hers, on a dry clear wintry morning, through the rarified air of these chalky hogs'-backs, was not depressing . . . In time she reached the edge of the vast escarpment below which stretched the loamy Vale of Blackmoor, now lying misty and still in the dawn. Instead of the colourless air of the uplands the atmosphere down there was a deep blue. Instead of the great enclosures of a hundred acres in which she was now accustomed to toil there were little fields below her of less than half-a-dozen acres, so numerous that they looked from this height like the meshes of a net. Here the landscape as whitey-brown; down there, as in the Froom Valley, it was always green. Yet it was in that vale that her sorrow had taken shape, and she did not love it as formerly. Beauty to her, as to all who have felt, lay not in the thing, but in what the thing symbolized.

—**Thomas Hardy,** *Tess of the D'Urbervilles*

Lancy, October 31, 1852.—A half hour's walk in the garden in a fine rain.—Autumnal landscape. The sky hung with various shades of gray, mists trailing over the mountains on the horizon; nature melancholy; leaves falling on all sides like the last illusions of youth under the tears of incurable sorrows.

—**Henri Frederic Amiel,** "What a Lovely Walk!"

The fire has gone out. The sun has gone down ever so slightly. I still want to walk a good distance today. As I begin packing and wrapping up my bundle, I think of another bit of Eichendorff, and I sing it on my knees:

Soon, oh how soon the still time will come,
When I too will rest, and over me
Will rustle the lovely loneliness of trees,
And, even here, no one will know me.

I perceive for the first time that even in this beloved passage the sadness is merely the shadow of a cloud. This sadness is nothing but the gentle music of passing things, and without it, whatever is beautiful does not touch us. It is without pain. I take it with me on my journey, and I feel contented as I step briskly farther up the mountain path, the lake far below me, past a mill brook with chestnut trees and a sleeping mill wheel, into the quiet blue day.

—**Hermann Hesse,** *Wandering*

When I walk
I part the air
and always
the air moves in
to fill the spaces
where my body's been.
—**Mark Strand,** "Reasons for Moving"

It so happens I am sick of being a man.
And it happens that I walk into tailorshops and movie houses
   dried up, waterproof, like a swan made of felt
   steering my way in a water of wombs and ashes.
—**Pablo Neruda,** "Walking Around"

Fear

Yea, though I walk through the valley of the shadow of death, I will fear no evil.

—**Psalms 23**

And they heard the voice of the Lord God walking in the garden in the cool of the day: and Adam and his wife hid themselves from the presence of the Lord God amongst the trees of the garden.

—**Genesis 3:8**

As a man who has come on a snake in the mountain valley suddenly steps back, and the shiver comes over his body, and he draws back and away, cheeks seized with a green pallor; so in terror of Atreus' son godlike Alexandros lost himself again in the host of the haughty Trojans.

—**Homer,** *The Iliad*

Come hither, you that walk along the way;
See how the pilgrims fare that go astray.
They catched are in an entangling net,
'Cause they good counsel lightly did forget:
'Tis true they rescued were, but yet you see,
They're scourged to boot. Let this your caution be.
—**John Bunyan,** *The Pilgrim's Progress*

Let constant vigilance thy footsteps guide,
And wary circumspection guard thy side;
Then shalt thou walk unharm'd the dang'rous night,
Nor need th' officious link-boy's smoaky light.
Thou never wilt attempt to cross the road,
Where alehouse benches rest the porter's load,
Grievous to heedless shins; no barrow's wheel,
That bruises oft' the truant school-boy's heel,
Behind thee rolling, with insidious pace,
Shall mark thy stocking with a miry trace.
Let not thy vent'rous steps approach too nigh,
Where gaping wide, low steepy cellars lie;
Should thy shoe wrench aside, down, down you fall,
And overturn the scolding huckster's stall,
The scolding huckster shall not o'er thee moan,
But pence exact for nuts and pears o'erthrown.
—**John Gay,** *Trivia; Or, The Art of Walking the*
Streets of London

I quitted my seat, and walked on, although the darkness
and storm increased every minute, and the thunder burst
with a terrific crash over my head. It was echoed from

Saleve, the Juras, and the Alps of Savoy; vivid flashes of lightning dazzled my eyes, illuminating the lake, making it appear like a vast sheet of fire; then for an instant every thing seemed of a pitchy darkness, until the eye recovered itself from the preceding flash. . . . While I watched the storm, so beautiful yet terrific, I wandered on with a hasty step. This noble war in the sky elevated my spirits; I clasped my hands and exclaimed aloud, "William, dear angel! this is thy funeral, this thy dirge!" As I said these words, I perceived in the gloom a figure which stole from behind a clump of trees near me; I stood fixed, gazing intently; I could not be mistaken. A flash of lightning illuminated the object, and discovered its shape plainly to me; its gigantic stature, and the deformity of its aspect, more hideous than belongs to humanity, instantly informed me that it was the wretch, the filthy daemon to whom I had given life.

—**Mary Shelley,** *Frankenstein*

I skirted fields, and hedges, and lanes, till after sunrise. I believe it was a lovely summer morning: I know my shoes, which I had put on when I left the house, were soon wet with dew. But I looked neither to rising sun, nor smiling sky, nor wakening nature. He who is taken out to pass through a fair scene to the scaffold thinks not of the flowers that smile on his road, but of the block and axe-edge; of the disseverment of bone and vein; of the grave gaping at the end: and I thought of drear flight and homeless wandering. . . .

—**Charlotte Brontë,** *Jane Eyre*

I choose to walk at all risks.

—**Elizabeth Barrett Browning,** *Aurora Leigh*

He went on doggedly; but as he left the town behind him, and plunged into the solitude and darkness of the road, he felt a dread and awe creeping upon him which shook him to the core. Every object before him, substance or shadow, still or moving, took the semblance of some fearful thing; but these fears were nothing compared to the sense that haunted him of that morning's ghastly figure following at his heels. He could trace its shadow in the gloom, supply the smallest item of the outline, and note how stiff and solemn it seemed to stalk along. He could hear its garments rustling in the leaves, and every breath of wind came laden with that last low cry. If he stopped it did the same. If he ran, it followed—not running too: that would have been a relief: but like a corpse endowed with the mere machinery of life, and borne on one slow melancholy wind that never rose or fell.

—**Charles Dickens,** *Oliver Twist*

(Bill Sykes fleeing the murder of Nancy)

It was something even more intense than despair that I then observed upon the countenance of the singular being whom I had watched so pertinaciously. Yet he did not hesitate in his career, but, with a mad energy, retraced his steps at once, to the heart of the mighty London. Long and swiftly he fled, while I followed him in the wildest amazement, resolute not to abandon a scrutiny in which I now felt an interest all-absorbing. The sun arose while we proceeded, and, when we had once again reached that most thronged mart of the populous town, the street of the D— Hotel, it presented an appearance of human bustle and activity scarcely inferior to what I had seen on the evening before. And here, long, amid the momently increasing confusion, did I persist in my pursuit of the stranger. But, as usual, he walked to and fro, and during the day did not pass from out the turmoil of that street. And, as the shades of the second evening came on, I grew wearied unto death, and, stopping fully in front of the wanderer, gazed at him steadfastly in the face. He noticed me not, but resumed his solemn walk, while I, ceasing to follow, remained absorbed in contemplation. "The old man," I said at length, "is the type and the genius of deep crime. He refuses to be alone. He is the man of the crowd. It will be in vain to follow, for I shall learn no more of him, nor of his deeds."

—**Edgar Allan Poe,** "The Man of the Crowd"

Did no men passing through the dim streets shrink without knowing why, when he came stealing up behind them? As he glided on, had no child in its sleep an indistinct perception of a guilty shadow falling on its bed, that troubled its innocent rest? Did no dog howl, and strive to break its rattling chain, that it might tear him; no burrowing rat, scenting the work he had in hand, essay to gnaw a passage after him, that it might hold a greedy revel at the feast of his providing? When he looked back, across his shoulder, was it to see if his quick footsteps still fell dry upon the dusty pavement, or were already moist and clogged with the red mire that stained the naked feet of Cain!

—**Charles Dickens,** *Martin Chuzzlewit*

Suppose one day the walking wouldn't stop,
became compulsive, step beyond step
and hours later it would be night and no longer
safe to be out.

—**Cole Swensen,** *Walk*

"Well, it was this way," returned Mr. Enfield: "I was coming home from some place at the end of the world, about three o'clock of a black winter morning, and my way lay through a part of town where there was literally nothing to be seen but lamps. Street after street, and all the folks asleep—street after street, all lighted up as if for a procession, and all as empty as a church—till at last I got into that state of mind when a man listens and listens and begins to long for the sight of a policeman. All at once, I saw two figures: one a little man who was stumping along eastward at a good walk, and the other a girl of maybe eight or ten who was running as hard as she was able down a cross-street. Well, sir, the two ran into one another naturally enough at the corner; and then came the horrible part of the thing; for the man trampled calmly over the child's body and left her screaming on the ground. It sounds nothing to hear, but it was hellish to see. It wasn't like a man; it was like some damned Juggernaut. I gave a halloa, took to my heels, collared my gentleman, and brought him back to where there was already quite a group about the screaming child. He was perfectly cool and made no resistance, but gave me one look, so ugly that it brought out the sweat on me like running."

—**Robert Louis Stevenson**, *The Strange Case of Dr. Jekyll and Mr. Hyde*

"You may go back to the hotel, Mother, but I'm going to take a walk," said Daisy.

"She's going to walk with Mr. Giovanelli," Randolph proclaimed.

"I am going to the Pincio," said Daisy, smiling.

"Alone, my dear—at this hour?" Mrs. Walker asked. The

afternoon was drawing to a close—it was the hour for the throng of carriages and of contemplative pedestrians. "I don't think it's safe, my dear," said Mrs. Walker.

—**Henry James,** *Daisy Miller*

Once he found himself almost into a swamp. He was obliged to walk upon bog tufts and watch his feet to keep from the oily mire. Pausing at one time to look about him he saw, out at some black water, a small animal pounce in and emerge directly with a gleaming fish.

The youth went again into the deep thickets. The brushed branches made a noise that drowned the sounds of cannon. He walked on, going from obscurity into promises of a greater obscurity.

At length he reached a place where the high, arching boughs made a chapel. He softly pushed the green doors aside and entered. Pine needles were a gentle brown carpet. There was a religious half light.

Near the threshold he stopped, horror-stricken at the sight of a thing.

He was being looked at by a dead man who was seated with his back against a columnlike tree. The corpse was dressed in a uniform that had once been blue, but was now faded to a melancholy shade of green. The eyes, staring at the youth, had changed to the dull hue to be seen on the side of a dead fish. The mouth was open. Its red had changed to an appalling yellow. Over the gray skin of the face ran little ants. One was trundling some sort of bundle along the upper lip.

The youth gave a shriek as he confronted the thing. He was for moments turned to stone before it. He remained staring into the liquid-looking eyes. The dead man and the living man exchanged a long look. Then the youth cautiously put one hand behind him and brought it against a tree. Leaning upon this he retreated, step by step, with his face still toward the thing. He feared that if he turned his back the body might spring up and stealthily pursue him.

The branches, pushing against him, threatened to throw him over upon it. His unguided feet, too, caught aggravatingly in brambles; and with it all he received a subtle suggestion to touch the corpse. As he thought of his hand upon it he shuddered profoundly.

At last he burst the bonds which had fastened him to the spot and fled, unheeding the underbrush. He was pursued by the sight of black ants swarming greedily upon the gray face and venturing horribly near to the eyes.

After a time he paused, and, breathless and panting, listened. He imagined some strange voice would come from the dead throat and squawk after him in horrible menaces.

The trees about the portal of the chapel moved soughingly in a soft wind. A sad silence was upon the little guarding edifice.

—**Stephen Crane,** *The Red Badge of Courage*

"There came to be" "a voice in" "my head" "always a faint voice" "that ordered me" "to keep walking" "from room to room" "'Keep walking,'" "keep walking," "it whispered" "as I approached" "what appeared to be" "a monstrous snake" "with a wide" "open mouth"

—**Alice Notley,** *the descent of Alette*

A sound of quick steps broke the silence of the moor. Crouching among the stones, we stared intently at the silver-tipped bank in front of us. The steps grew louder, and through the fog, as through a curtain, there stepped the man whom we were awaiting. He looked round him in surprise as he emerged into the clear, star-lit night. Then he came swiftly along the path, passed close to where we lay, and went on up the long slope behind us. As we walked he glanced continually over either shoulder, like a man who is ill at ease.

"Hist!" cried Holmes, and I heard the sharp click of a cocking pistol. "Look out! It's coming!"

There was a thin, crisp, continuous patter from somewhere in the heart of that crawling bank. The cloud was within fifty yards of where we lay, and we glared at it, all three, uncertain what horror was about to break from the heart of it. I was at Holmes's elbow, and I glanced for an instant at his face. It was pale and exultant, his eyes shining brightly in the moonlight. But suddenly they started forward in a rigid, fixed stare, and his lips parted in amazement. At the same instant Lestrade gave a yell of terror and threw himself face downwards upon the ground. I sprang to my feet, my inert hand grasping my pistol, my mind paralyzed by the dreadful shape which had sprung out upon us from the shadows of the fog. A hound it was, an enormous coal-black hound, but not such a hound as mortal eyes have ever seen. Fire burst from its open mouth, its eyes glowed with a smouldering glare, its muzzle and hackles and dewlap were outlined in flickering flame. Never in the delirious dream of a disordered brain could anything more savage, more appalling, more hellish, be conceived than that dark form and savage face which broke upon us out of the wall of fog.

—**Arthur Conan Doyle,** *The Hound of the Baskervilles*

as with the boy—or man—who had climbed the flag-pole to get away from the cops. I was walking home—he'd been hit by a club—foam came out of his mouth

—**Leslie Scalapino,** "Walking By"

About five o' clock I was off ahead and noticed a path which I had been told I should meet with, and, when met with, I must follow. The path was slightly indistinct, but by keeping my eye on it I could see it. Presently I came to a place where it went out, but appeared again on the other side of a clump of underbrush fairly distinctly. I made a short cut for it and the next news was I was in a heap, on a lot of spikes, some fifteen feet or so below ground level, at the bottom of a bag-shaped game pit.

It is at these times you realise the blessing of a good thick skirt. Had I paid heed to the advice of many people in England, who ought to have known better, and did not do it themselves, and adopted masculine garments, I should have been spiked to the bone, and done for. Whereas, save for a good many bruises, here I was with the fulness of my skirt tucked under me, sitting on nine ebony spikes some twelve inches long, in comparative comfort. . . .

—**Mary Kingsley,** *Travels in West Africa*

Every neighborhood has bullies, and I'm convinced that they watch how we walk. In Forest Hills, shufflers were in deep trouble, as were the pigeon-toed. Kids who walked like ducks were doomed. (Girls always were in some danger no matter how they walked, but that's another subject, too large and complicated to discuss here.) Kids who bounced when they walked were in less trouble, but rarely were taken seriously. A loose-limbed, jaunty, I'm-cool kind of walk almost always signaled someone who talked too much. He'd get in trouble with his mouth. And a straight, ramrod-up-the-ass walk suggested either terror of simply being alive, or some desperate need to be in control, which probably amount to the same thing. Bullies would flick lighted matches at those kids, would try to make them dance on command. . . . I tried to cultivate a walk that would give away none of the above. I think my walk was somewhere in between "walking tall," like the best movie heroes, and walking quietly, like a medium-sized animal, a vegetarian, trying not to disturb his natural enemy.

—**Stephen Dunn,** "Stepping Out"

Up the street hunting parties are abroad, whom the walker must take cognizance of; it's not enough to have your historical guidebook and go maundering about to the Old Merchant's House on East Fourth Street. A pair of bravos will ask you for a light and want a light; another pair, when your hands are in your pockets, will slug you. If you're lucky they will slug you; the old bar fighters complain about how risky fighting has become. You must have a considerable feel for these things, an extra sense, eyes in the back of your head: or call it a walker's *emotional range.* You must know when a pistol pointed at you playfully by a ten-year-old is a cap pistol and when it's not; whether someone coming toward you with a broken bottle is really going for you or not. . . . Now, muggers are herd creatures like the rest of us; they too have a "rush hour." So if a walker is indeed an individualist there is nowhere he can't go at dawn and not many places he can't go at noon. But just as it demeans life to live alongside a great river you can no longer swim in or drink from, to be crowded into the safer areas and hours takes much of the gloss off of walking—one sport you shouldn't have to reserve a time and a court for.

—**Edward Hoagland,** "City Walking"

The shadow walked on the earth like an animal; the grass was flattened; the sandy stretches smoked. The shadow walked on its supple legs. There it was, old and heavy on one's shoulders. No sound. It went its way. It passed by; that was all.

—**Jean Giono,** *Harvest*

The way is so narrow at times that the willow trunks simultaneously rub both ends of the rolled pad on the top of my pack.

Like an explosion in my face, a grouse starts up, two feet away, whirring. I break out in muskeg, back to heavy woods. I have a metal cup. I tap on it with a spoon. I pass bear scat, old and familiar. Tap. Now another mound. I have not seen that one before. Tap. Tap. In other words, never surprise a bear. One or two *must* be here somewhere. To make myself known, I deliver lectures to them in a voice designed to clear the hall. "Uncontrolled fear and deep respect are two different things," I explain to them. "You've got to have a healthy respect for what comes through the country." . . .

I embrace this wild country. But how can I be of it, how can I move within it? I can't accept anymore the rationale of the few who go unarmed—yet I am equally loath to use guns. If bears were no longer in the country, I would not have come. I am here, in a sense, because they survive. So I am sorry—truly rueful and perplexed—that without a means of killing them I cannot feel at ease.

—**John McPhee,** *Coming into the Country*

Being born a woman is my awful tragedy. Yes, my consuming desire to mingle with road crews, sailors and soldiers, barroom regulars—to be part of a scene, anonymous, listening, recording—all is spoiled by the fact that I am a girl, a female always in danger of assault and battery. My consuming interest in men and their lives is often misconstructed as a desire to seduce them, or as an invitation to intimacy. Yes, God, I want to talk to everybody I can as deeply as I can. I want to be able to sleep in an open field, to travel west, to walk freely at night.

—**Sylvia Plath,** journal

Lila walked in the streets like someone who had always walked in the streets and for whom it was natural and rich. She walked with the illusion that she was safe and that the illusion would somehow keep her that way. Yet, that particular night as she went out for cigarettes, Lila walked uneasily, her mind wandering until it stopped of its own accord on the simple fact that she was not safe. She could be physically hurt at any time and felt, for a fleeting moment, that she would be. She sat on the trunk of a '74 Chevy and accepted that this world was not hers. Even on her own block.

—**Sarah Schulman,** *Girls, Visions and Everything*

Freedom

If you are ready to leave father and mother, and brother and sister, and wife and child and friends, and never see them again,—if you have paid your debts, and made your will, and settled all your affairs, and are a free man, then you are ready for a walk.

—Henry David Thoreau, "Walking"

The soul of a journey is liberty, perfect liberty, to think, feel, do just as one pleases. We go a journey chiefly to be free of all impediments and of all inconveniences; to leave ourselves behind, much more to get rid of others.

—**William Hazlitt,** "On Going a Journey"

The World was all before them, where to choose
Thir place of rest, and Providence thir guide:
They hand in hand with wandring steps and slow
Through Eden took thir solitary way.

—**John Milton,** *Paradise Lost*

O welcome messenger! O welcome friend!
A captive greets thee, coming from a house
Of bondage, from your city's walls set free,
A prison where he hath been long immured.
Now I am free, enfranchised and at large,
May fix my habitation where I will.
What dwelling shall receive me? In what Vale

Shall be my harbour? Under what grove
Shall I take up my home, and what sweet stream
Shall with its murmurs lull me to my rest?
The earth is all before me: with a heart
Joyous, or scared at its own liberty,
I look about, and should the guide I chuse
Be nothing better than a wandering cloud,
I cannot miss my way.
—**William Wordsworth,** *The Prelude*

Afoot and light-hearted I take to the open road,

Healthy, free, the world before me,

The long brown path before me leading wherever I choose.

—**Walt Whitman,** "Song of the Open Road"

Afoot and in the open road, one has a fair start in life at last. There is no hindrance now. Let him put his best foot forward. He is on the broadest human plane. This is on the level of all the great laws and heroic deeds. From this platform he is eligible to any good fortune. He was sighing for the golden age; let him walk to it.

—**John Burroughs,** "The Exhilarations of the Road"

The man was wild
And wandered. His home was where he was free.
Everybody has met one such man as he.
Does he keep clear old paths that no one uses
But once a lifetime when he loves or muses?

—**Edward Thomas,** "Lob"

the walk liberating, I was released from forms,
from the perpendiculars,
    straight lines, blocks, boxes, binds
of thought
into the hues, shadings, rises, flowing bends and blends
    of sight:

—**A. R. Ammons,** "Corsons Inlet"

A walk expresses space and freedom and the knowledge of it can live in the imagination of anyone, and that is another space too.

—**Richard Long,** "Five Six Pick Up Sticks,
Seven Eight Lay Them Straight"

We saw some sheep
take a walk in their sleep.
By the light of the moon,
by the light of a star,
they walked all night
from near to far."

—**Dr. Seuss,** *One Fish, Two Fish, Red Fish, Blue Fish*

In the pines
He is merry, he's free.
He sleeps, he walks

—**Louis Zukofsky,** "A"-12

As I went walking
That ribbon of highway
I saw above me
That endless skyway.
I saw below me
The lonesome valley.
This land was made for you and me.
—**Woody Guthrie,** "This Land Is Your Land"

Bibliography

Walking anthologies

Belloc, Hillare, ed. *The Footpath Way.* 1911.

Goldmark, Pauline and Mary Hopkins, eds. *The Gypsy Trail: An Anthology for Campers.* 1922.

Goodman, George. *The Lore of the Wanderer: An Open-Air Anthology.* 1920.

Graham, Stephen, ed. *The Gentle Art of Tramping.* New York: D. Appleton & Co., 1926.

Mitchell, Edwin Valentine, ed. *The Pleasures of Walking.* 1934.

Sidgwick, A. H., ed. *Walking Essays.* London: Edward Arnold, 1912.

Sussman, Aaron and Ruth Goode, eds. *The Magic of Walking.* New York: Simon and Schuster, 1967.

Trent, George D., ed. *The Gentle Art of Walking.* New York: Arno–Random House, 1971.

Wellman, Angelika, ed. *Der Spaziergang:* Ein Literarisches Lesebuch. Olms, 1992.

Zochert, Donald, ed. *Walking in America.* New York: Alfred A. Knopf, 1974.

Literary and Historical Studies

Barta, Peter I., *Bely, Joyce, and Doblin: Peripatetics in the City Novel.* Gainesville: University of Florida Press, 1996.

Benjamin, Walter. *Charles Baudelaire: A Lyric Poet in the Era of High Capitalism.* Trans. Harry Zohn. London: New Left Books, 1973.

Brand, Dana. *The Spectator and the City in Nineteenth-Century American Literature.* Cambridge, U.K.: Cambridge University Press, 1991.

Bushnell, Nelson S. *A Walk After John Keats.* New York: Farrar & Rineholt, 1936.

Cohen, Margaret. *Profane Illumination: Walter Benjamin and the Paris of Surrealist Revolution.* University of California Press, 1993.

Cummings, John. *Runners and Walkers: A Nineteenth-Century Sports Chronicle.* Chicago: Regnery Gateway, 1981.

Elder, John. *Imagining the Earth: Poetry and the Vision of Nature.* Urbana and Chicago: University of Illlinois Press, 1985.

Chambers, Ross. *Loiterature.* Lincoln: University of Nebraska Press, 1999.

Gleber, Anke. *The Art of Taking a Walk: Flanerie, Literature and Film in Weimar Culture.* Princeton, NJ: Princeton University Press, 1999.

Gilbert, Roger. *Walks in the World: Representation and Experience in Modern American Poetry.* Princeton, NJ: Princeton University Press, 1991.

Holmes, Richard. *Footsteps: Adventures of a Romantic Biographer.* New York: Viking, 1985.

Jarvis, Robin. *Romantic Writing and Pedestrian Travel.* Houndsmill and London: Macmillian; New York: St. Martins, 1997.

Jusserand, J. J. *English Wayfaring Life in the Middle Ages.* London: T. Fisher Unwin, 1888.

Langan, Celeste. *Romantic Vagrancy: Wordsworth and the Simulation of Freedom.* Cambridge: Cambridge University Press, 1996.

Marples, Morris. *Shanks's Pony: A Study of Walking.* London: J.M. Dent & Sons, 1959.

Nord, Deborah Epstein. *Walking the Victorian Streets: Women, Representation and the City.* Ithaca and New York: Cornell University Press, 1995.

Robinson, Jeffrey. *The Walk: Notes on a Romantic Image.* Norman: University of Oklahoma Press, 1989.

Solnit, Rebecca. *Wanderlust: A History of Walking.* New York: Viking, 2000.

Strickland, Ron. *Shank's Mare: A Compendium of Remarkable Walks.* New York: Paragon House, 1988.

Taplin, Kim. *The English Path.* Woodbridge, Suffolk: The Boydell Press, 1979.

Wallace, Anne D. *Walking, Literature, and English Culture: The Origin and Uses of Peripatetic in the Nineteenth Century.* Oxford: Clarendon, 1993.

Index

(Page given is the opening page of quote. Some quotes may run over to the next page.)

Elder, John (American critic, b. 1947), 139
Eliot, George (English novelist, 1819-1880), 88, 217
Eliot, T. S. (American poet and critic, 1886-1965), 66
Eluard, Paul (French poet, 1895-1952), 121
Emerson, Ralph Waldo (American essayist and poet, 1803-1882), 59, 63, 86
Fairburn, A. R. D. (New Zealand poet, 1904-1957), 32
Ferlinghetti, Lawrence (American poet, b. 1919), 125
Ficino, Marsilio (Italian philosopher, 1433-1499), 171
Fielding, Henry (English novelist, 1707-1754), 172
Forster, E. M. (English novelist, 1879-1970), 53
France, Anatole (French novelist, 1844-1824), 23
Freud, Sigmund (German psychologist, 1856-1939), 136
Frey, Nancy (American historian, b. 1968), 22
Frost, Robert (American poet, 1875-1962), 48, 67, 98, 176
Gaskell, Elizabeth (English novelist and biographer, 1810-1865), 189
Gay, John (English poet and playwright, 1685-1732), 118, 225
Genesis, 224
Giacometti, Alberto (Swiss sculptor, 1901-1966), 197
Ginsberg, Allen (American poet, 1926-1998), 67, 192
Ginzburg, Natalia (Italian novelist, 1916-1991), 35
Giono, Jean (French novelist, 1895-1970), 239
Giovanni, Nikki (American poet, b. 1943), 126
Goethe, Johann Wolfgang von (German poet and novelist, 1749-1832), 17
Goldsmith, Oliver (English poet and novelist, 1730-1774), 61
Graham, Stephen (American essayist, 1884-1975), 16
Gray, Thomas (English poet, 1716-1771), 60
Griffith, Richard M. (American philosopher, b. 1921), 32
Grossman, Allen (American poet and critic, b. 1932), 138
Gumilev, Nikolai S. (Russian poet, 1886-1921), 175
Guthrie, Woody (American folk songwriter, 1912-1967), 248
Hamill, Sam (American poet and translator, b. 1943), 96
Handy, W. C. (American blues composer, 1873-1958), 176
Hardy, Thomas (English poet and novelist, 1840-1928), 218
Hawthorne, Nathaniel (American novelist, 1804-1864), 85, 103
Hazlitt, William (English essayist, 1778-1830), 134, 142, 154, 207, 244
Hejinian, Lyn (American poet, b. 1941), 212
Herzog, Werner (German filmmaker, b. 1942), 47, 160
Hesse, Hermann (German novelist, 1877-1962), 220
Hessel, Franz (German novelist, 1880-1941), 111
Hiss, Tony (American essayist, b. 1942), 165
Hoagland, Edward (American essayist, b. 1932), 20, 238
Hogan, Linda (American poet and essayist, b. 1947), 70
Holmes, Richard (English biographer, b. 1945) 194,
Homer (Greek poet, c. 800 B.C.), 224

Nabokov, Vladimir (Russian-American novelist, 1899-1977), 94, 160
Napier, John (American anthropologist, 1917-1987), 29
Navajo tribe, 208
Neruda, Pablo (Chilean poet, 1904-1973), 221
Nicolson, Adam (English travel writer, b. 1957), 19
Nietzsche, Friedrich (German philosopher, 1844-1900), 136
Notley Alice (American poet, b. 1945), 234
O'Hara, Frank (American poet, 1926-1966), 127
Oliver, Mary (American poet, b. 1935) 49
Palazzeschi, Aldo (Italian poet, 1885-1974), 57
Paracelsus (German philosopher, 1493-1541), 13
Petrarch, Francesco (Italian poet, 1304-1374), 171
Piercy, Marge (American poet, b. 1936), 46
Plath, Sylvia (American poet, 1932-1963), 241
Plato (Greek philosopher, 427-347 B.C.), 38
Poe, Edgar Allan (American poet and fiction writer, 1809-1849), 228
Pope, Alexander (English poet, 1688-1744), 202
Pritchett, V.S. (English writer, 1900-1997), 74
Proust, Marcel (French novelist, 1871-1922), 43
Radbertus, Paschasius (French theologian, 786-860), 214
Renard, Jules (French playwright and essayist, 1864-1910), 138, 161
Rexroth, Kenneth (American poet, 1905-1982) 46
Reznikoff, Charles (American poet, 1894-1976) 67, 108, 124
Riding, Laura (American poet and philosopher, 1901-1991), 138
Roethke, Theodore (American poet, 1908-1963), 55
Rousseau, Jean-Jacques (French philosopher), 131, 133
Ruiz, Raul (Spanish novelist, b. 1941), 47
Sackville-West, Vita (English poet and novelist, 1892-1962), 203
Scalapino, Leslie (American poet, b. 1947), 236
Schulman, Sarah (American novelist, b. 1958), 241
Dr. Seuss (Theodor Seuss Geisel—American children's book author and artist, 1904-1991), 247
Shakespeare, William (English playwright and poet, 1564-1616), 39, 214
Shelley, Mary (English novelist, 1797-1850), 215, 225
Smith, Charlotte (English poet, 1749-1806), 39, 82, 100
Snyder, Gary (American poet and essayist, b. 1929), 28, 94, 192
Socrates (Greek philosopher), 38
Song of Solomon, 169
Soupault, Philippe (French poet and novelist, 1897-1990), 65, 122
Spenser, Edmund (English poet, 1552-1599), 100
Sphinx, 26
Stendhal (French novelist, 1783-1842), 196
Stephen, Leslie (English essayist, 1832-1904), 7, 15, 136, 185
Stern, Gerald (American poet, b. 1925), 99